D1153922

THOMAS MIDDLETON
AND THE
DRAMA OF REALISM

THOMAS MIDDLETON
and the
Drama of Realism

A Study of
Some Representative Plays

DOROTHY M. FARR

OLIVER & BOYD · EDINBURGH

First published in 1973 by
OLIVER AND BOYD
Croythorn House
23 Ravelston Terrace
Edinburgh EH4 3TJ
A Division of Longman Group Limited

ISBN 0 05 002607 0

Printed in Great Britain by
Western Printing Services Ltd,
Bristol

To My Mother

Contents

Acknowledgements

I should like to express my thanks to Professor Kenneth Muir who kindly read and advised upon the typescript in its original form, to the Modern Humanities Research Association and the Editors of the Modern Language Review for permission to reprint in Chapter 4 the greater part of an article on *The Changeling* first published in the Modern Language Review 62 (1967) pp. 586–597, and lastly to Catherine Parry for unfailing counsel and encouragement and much tolerance!

NOTE: All references for quotations from the works of Middleton, Rowley and Webster, are to the following editions:

The Works of Thomas Middleton, ed. A. H. Bullen (8 vols). London, 1885–6.
William Rowley: His 'All's Lost by Lust' and 'A Shoemaker a Gentleman', ed. C. W. Stork. Philadelphia, 1910.
The Works of John Webster, ed. F. L. Lucas. London, 1927.

1. Introduction

AMONG the later Jacobean dramatists Middleton seems to stand alone. He made little mark on contemporary drama, yet there is about his work something rare and challenging which time does not stale. His knowledge and understanding of his own theatre were evidently thorough and instinctive, but he could have been at home in a much later one; he could follow a literary fashion without surrendering his own individuality, he could write with poets as dissimilar as Dekker and Webster, he could absorb any influence that came his way, yet he was never committed to any one of them and none of the familiar categories will fit him. Some of his greatest work was written in collaboration, but even then it is seldom possible to discern his hand with certainty and the problem of dating his work is equally difficult. With Middleton elusiveness, a kind of anonymity, seems to be a basic characteristic.

Now this detachment has created a certain barrier between Middleton and his critics. To some extent Eliot's well known comment has coloured his reputation: 'He has no point of view . . . He has no message; he is merely a great recorder.'[1] Recent studies have modified this opinion yet Middleton is still, even to his warmest admirers, as isolated as he probably was in his own time—an outsider whom no one would follow. Mr. Tomlinson's phrase—'The uncharacteristic Jacobean'[2]—accurately describes his position, for while he was a man of his age and probably understood its social and moral dilemma and the strains that the future might put upon it, as few of his contemporaries did, he was unique even in that understanding.

Middleton's 'message' is contained in his irony; it is an irony born of the equivocal view of life which for Middleton was basic to the human comedy. Part of his distinction was in using this irony not merely to illumine a particular theme or define a situation, though it could often do both, but as the core and shaping impulse of a whole play. Combined with a natural

1

immediacy of dialogue and manner which often comes near to
Shakespeare, it enabled him to penetrate character and situation
always objectively, but with an acuteness which involves the
audience at depth, so that in his greatest plays comedy and
tragedy flow into one another as they do in life. Now this demanded a new kind of drama, and in succeeding chapters I have
tried to show how Middleton was feeling his way towards a new
vehicle. His death in 1627 leaving to represent his mature achievement only one tragedy in its entirety, written during a brief
phase of greatness after 1620, was a loss to the English theatre.
It was with the close of Middleton's career, not with that of
Ford's, that Elizabethan tragedy came to its end. Those who
appreciate Middleton's work and his place in the history of the
English theatre may regret that he did not live long enough to
establish a mode in which other dramatists could have followed
him.

It may be true that at any rate during the first half of his
career he regarded the theatre primarily as a means of livelihood
and cared little, on the whole, for his reputation as an artist. It
is certainly true that in collaboration he was content to sink his
genius in that of his colleagues if the play and theatre business
demanded it. For this reason it is useless to look for sustained
trends of development in these years. Certain influences are
traceable and sometimes formative, but Middleton's early and
middle career is a series of flat levels, probably determined as
much by the situation in the theatre as by any clearly defined
artistic purpose.

He was a Londoner, born of a middle-class family about 1680,
probably educated at Queen's College, Oxford, and less certainly
at an Inn of Court.[3] He began to write in his student days and
probably like other poets who found themselves, partly against
their will, in the theatre, he saw himself first as a poet and satirist.
At seventeen he produced a verse rendering of *The Wisdom of
Solomon* and two years later, *Micro-Cynicon, or Six Snarling
Satires* which may have owed something to Dekker's satirical
pamphlets.[4] *The Black Book* and *Father Hubbard's Tale* followed
in 1604, both satirical, both descriptive of London life and the
evils of the world of his day.

Perhaps it was this budding gift for satire, and for the observation of life which is a requisite for it, that drew him to Dekker and

Webster—and faced him with the hard facts of theatre life as Henslowe understood it, for in 1602 the latter records payment to Middleton for his work in *Caesar's Fall*, now lost, in which both Dekker and Webster collaborated. Equally important is this first record for its evidence of his association with the Admiral's Men who staged the play, for later in 1603–4, when they became Prince Henry's Men, the same company also staged Dekker's play *The Honest Whore* in which Middleton was again collaborating. This was a play which he was not to forget, for his own comedy of London, *The Roaring Girl* of 1607, to which Dekker contributed, was written in the same spirit and tradition. Both plays are concerned not only with citizen life but with the struggles and perplexities of recognisable human beings in a society as harsh as it was lively.

By 1603–4 however another phase in Middleton's career as a dramatist had begun, for he was already writing for a different type of theatre—the private theatre of the two leading children's companies, the Boys of St. Paul's and the Children of the Chapel Royal, later the Revels Company, in the new indoor theatre at Blackfriars. He has been credited with *Blurt Master Constable*, played at St. Paul's in 1602, and in 1603–4, the year of *The Black Book* and *Father Hubbard's Tale*, he found another outlet for moral satire in *The Phoenix*. For the next five years he wrote primarily, though towards the end of the period not entirely, for the Children's Companies. *A Trick to Catch the Old One*, *A Mad World my Masters*, *Michaelmas Term* and *The Puritan* were all staged at St. Paul's between 1604 and 1607, and *The Family of Love*, *Your Five Gallants* and most probably *The Widow*, though this play is of less certain date, at Blackfriars between 1604 and 1608.[5]

These five years of work in the two principal private theatres were a period of training which was to bear fruit in Middleton's later plays. No doubt his taste for satire as well as practical considerations drew him to the lucrative but restricting task of writing for the Children's Companies. For the Children he could write satirical comedy quickly and easily; he knew how to please the fashionable audiences and could provide suitable material for the skilled boys who played before them. Returns were good, and one unfailing characteristic in Middleton at this period was his eye to business and to public demand and response. Comedy after comedy followed a similar pattern—indeed a good deal of his work can be regarded as variation on a theme—until about 1608–9. But from about 1606 the Children's Companies began to decline; they were discontinued after 1609 so that there is good reason for taking that year as a turning point in Middleton's life. Force of circumstances if nothing else, may have caused him to return to the popular theatre, and after 1608 we find him writing a broader type of comedy mainly for the adult players, and in particular for the Prince's and the Lady Elizabeth's Men.

This third phase covered roughly the next ten years and it was a busy period. Middleton was now established as one of the well known dramatists of his time; hitherto he had been following a type of drama in which Jonson was master; now it was behind him and so were the compulsion of a fashion and the restriction of writing for a small exclusive audience. The theatre for which he now mainly worked was the theatre of poet-dramatists like his old associates Dekker and Webster. Perhaps the earliest indication of Webster's influence is in *A Chaste Maid in Cheapside* of about 1613, written for the Lady Elizabeth's Men and acted at the Swan, and also by the Revels Company who still functioned intermittently at Blackfriars. It was during these years that Middleton developed his interest in women characters, for instance in *A Fair Quarrel* and *No Wit no Help like a Woman's*. Somewhere during this period came *The Witch*, the play containing the witches' song which found its way into later performances of *Macbeth*, and *More Dissemblers Besides Women*. But the most important event in this phase of Middleton's career was the recommencement of his association with William Rowley in *A Fair Quarrel* of about 1615. Precisely what Rowley brought to Middleton it is impossible to assess. There are those who believe he contributed nothing more than revision while others would make of him at least a very considerable partner.[7] What we do know is that Rowley was essentially a man of the theatre who knew how to capture the interest of a popular audience with physical action as well as wit, and that it was while he was working with Rowley that Middleton produced some of his greatest writing in tragedy—itself a new venture for him—in *The Changeling* of about 1620–21.[8] This play marked the opening of the final brief, but greatest, phase in which he also produced unaided *Women Beware Women*, his last tragedy, and the political satire *A Game at Chess*.

The importance of *A Fair Quarrel* is in its near tragic content, the absence in it of the mordant satire of such plays as *A Trick* and *A Chaste Maid* and some evidence not only of the lead of Fletcher but of deviation from it. It is at this point that a clearer artistic purpose seems to emerge in Middleton's work. Henceforth the conventional comic intrigue centring upon citizen cupidity is relegated to the secondary plot, while the major interest becomes increasingly psychological.

After *The Changeling* Middleton seems to have written for the stage at more leisurely intervals. He was now frequently involved in commissioned writing for civic occasions and was responsible for a number of masques and entertainments. It may well be that financial need, perhaps as a result of the discontinuance of the Children's companies, compelled him to accept occasional work. He was appointed City Chronologer in 1620 and in the following year he was again collaborating with Webster in *Anything for a Quiet Life* for the King's Men in their winter quarters at Backfriars. But if his work for the stage was rarer it had the confidence of maturity, with the enrichment that experience of life in the theatre, perhaps also in civic connections, had given him. *Women Beware Women* was the clearest product of that experience, a play difficult to date but probably written sometime in 1624.[9] In the same year occurred the scandal connected with *A Game at Chess*, the play in which, not content with exposing a number of public personages, Middleton also included a sly hit at Philip of Spain. His adroitness in 'shifting out of the way'[10] did not save him from a brief period of imprisonment during which his son Edward Middleton appeared on his behalf before the Privy Council. But as far as Middleton was personally concerned no great damage had been done. He had written a play that was the talk of London during its phenomenal nine days' run and afterwards when it rushed into print, and he must have had some share in the returns, which were considerable while they lasted. The poor circumstances in which he left his widow at his death three years later do not necessarily suggest professional disappointment. He had never been part of a trend for longer than he found it useful, and he may well have seemed an independent rather than a popular figure in later years. Yet he had established himself as satirist and dramatist and had been associated with the most frequented private and popular theatres and with the leading companies of his day.

We know enough of Middleton's life to fill in the background of his professional experience, yet few dramatists have hidden themselves so effectually in their work. The bare facts suggest substance and middle-class respectability, yet he evidently knew poverty and low life equally well. The streets, the inns, the dark alleyways by the river, the haunts of watermen—all the daily goings-on of London life—he knew and could write of with relish. He had the trained observer's eye for detail, of manner, behaviour and locality, and what he could not recall from actual experience he could translate into familiar terms with the help of reading and surmise. That he preferred to present what he had seen may be assumed from the comparative absence of garden walks and open spaces, and the frequency of interiors and street corners, often circumstantially referred to, as background for his scene. All this may be a reflection of his own environment; on the other hand it would be difficult to find a single thought or opinion that we can attribute with any certainty to the dramatist himself. As for the characters and what they stand for, his detachment is absolute. Few writers have displayed so little partiality for their creations as they pass through their hands; neither praise nor blame was any part of Middleton's business. Middleton was a natural demonstrator, and having demonstrated from life in the raw he was too great an artist, and perhaps too great a teacher (for those who look for lessons in art) to betray his own position. Dogmatism is rare in his plays and the summaries at the close of the two late tragedies are no more than pointers to the pattern of the preceding action. Yet moral assumptions are firmly worked into the background of his characteristic work and the same assumptions remain with us when the play is over.

Years of work in satirical comedy, largely for the private theatre, had taught him the habit of succinctness, of fastidious under-statement, habits which can be stabilised only by unremitting attention in the poet himself. Thus his flair for essentials impelled him to jettison anything which he found irrelevant to meaning—and meaning as opposed to feeling—and his writing often has an attenuated, two-dimensional effect in consequence.

But we are apt to assume too easily that the austerity we find in his plays was fundamental to his thinking. He had chosen to write through formative years for a satirical purpose which in itself entailed selection, and he had allowed himself little time or space for outlet in sonnets or shorter poems; yet the rare occurrences of figurative poetry in the later plays, in *Women Beware Women* for instance, and the unloosing of a spontaneous lyricism in *A Game at Chess*, suggest a side of Middleton's gift for which the earlier comedies had not provided sufficient scope. Approximately after 1621 however, the outlook is both more purposeful and more imaginatively creative, as if the poet felt an inner release or some new and deeper inspiration. It is possible that Middleton's eye for expediency and his artist's vision were never entirely reconciled, yet from their adjustment there grew up a finely trained gift which unfortunately time cut short. But although his last period of mature achievement was short-lived, in the three last plays written after 1621 he could display a range and variety combined with a steadiness of vision in which few poet-dramatists can rival him.

Important as was Middleton's contribution to Jacobean tragedy his genius was essentially comic,[11] and as I have tried to show in later chapters, the uniqueness of his tragedies derives a good deal from his ability to develop an inherently comic situation at depth. With a writer so adaptable and so responsive to demand it is easy to find comparisons and a number are suggested in this book. But the familiar parallel with Restoration Comedy is especially apt. Indeed Middleton's plays often seem to look forward to a world in which he might have been better placed than in that of his contemporaries—a society in which values had become too complicated for dogmatism and the moral level too general for distinction between man and man. The view of life projected in his plays is of a vast network of intrigue in which men are trapped and trap one another. The trap which De Flores sets for Beatrice in *The Changeling*, Livia's deceptions in *Women Beware Women*, are designed to exploit their victims' weaknesses, even at times their pretensions to respectability; nevertheless they are foreshadowed in the tricksters' gambles of the earlier comedies. Indeed the game, whether of chance or skill, is for Middleton a basic concept. In *A Chaste Maid in Cheapside* the characters are gamesters to one another, and the plots of his plays are composed of tricks and counter-tricks, which are all subsumed in the game of chess which was perhaps the last and completest symbol in his work of the world as he conceived it. The uniqueness of Middleton is the unexpected depth and variety of experience which he finds in commonplace characters and situations, and the delicacy and forthrightness with which that experience is conveyed. He was never less than a theatre man and he knew how to give his dialogue that additional twist that jerks an audience into attention and often makes comedy indistinguishable from tragedy.

Of the seven plays selected for detailed consideration in this book, the three early comedies—*A Trick to Catch the Old One*, *The Widow*, and *A Chaste Maid in Cheapside*—are typical of his work for the Children's companies, but they also bear some clear indications of his later development, and the last, *A Chaste Maid*, marks the close of his early work. A separate short chapter is devoted to *A Fair Quarrel* which stands alone as a play of transition in which Middleton was ridding himself of earlier influences and moving towards a type of tragedy peculiarly his own. The chapters on the three last plays—*The Changeling*, *Women Beware Women* and *A Game at Chess*—I have placed in what I believe to be their probable date order.

Middleton's gift was slighter than Shakespeare's or Webster's or Jonson's, yet he had something which neither Webster nor Jonson possessed and which Shakespeare came too early to develop. Given Shakespeare's sustained energy and professional purpose his mature contribution to the drama might have emerged sooner and the Jacobean theatre would have been the sounder for it.

2. Early Comedy

MIDDLETON was not alone in choosing to write mainly for the Children's Companies during his formative years. The prejudice of middle-class Puritanism combined with periodic outbreaks of plague was making the public theatre an increasingly precarious source of livelihood. But the private theatres which housed the Children's Companies had an autonomy of their own. As Professor Harbage suggests,[1] the atmosphere of the Blackfriars theatre must have been rather that of a banqueting hall in a great house than of a public inn or bear garden, which the public open theatres probably still resembled. It was a small audience, numbering about 600, seated in a rectangular auditorium, perhaps round three sides of the stage. The general conditions in the private theatres probably made for intimacy and high prices must have determined the social level to some degree.

The reactions of a small select audience could be judged fairly accurately beforehand, and although interference from the censor was not infrequent and was often well-deserved, the dramatists' willingness to take risks suggests that the Children's Companies were, on the whole, more privileged than the adult troupes. Plays were, of course, sometimes transferred from one type of theatre to another, but the private theatre was the author's sphere; while the established companies of adult players were accustomed to making their own demands upon their author, the boys of St. Paul's or Blackfriars were ready material for an experienced dramatist to work with.

To write for the Children's Companies was to write for a team. This was not the theatre of well known figures such as Burbage or Alleyn; there were outstanding boy actors like Jonson's Saloman Pavey, but a year or two saw the end of their usefulness and they could not in any case dominate an audience as an adult actor might. It is noticeable that the comedies which Jonson and Middleton wrote for the children generally provide for balanced groups of characters, mainly on a level, while the action is

9

managed with a speed and economy which allows scope for the music, pageantry and dancing in which the boys were skilled and carefully trained.

So repetitive is the basic pattern of Middleton's comedies of this period that it seems obvious that he was writing for an audience which knew what it wanted and expected to have it constantly repeated. Clever gibes at the citizen or at popular religious sects and their middle-class following were an excuse for bawdry and frankly pornographic witticisms, and for a light-hearted acceptance of a sphere of life a degree removed from respectability. All this Middleton, like Jonson or Chapman, could produce with facility, but it is worth noting that what these plays lose in profundity they gain in technique. The ingenuities of the plot, the balance and succinctness of the dialogue—an artistry which has some affinity with that of classical comedy—were to have a lasting effect on his work. Middleton's plays for the Children are comedies of situation; it is not the characters but the complex of circumstances in which they find themselves that dominates the theme and provides the entertainment. Two or more groups of people engage in a series of intrigues; generally one group is led by youth, the other by age, as in *A Mad World my Masters*, where Follywit plays upon the snobbish vanity of his grandfather, Sir Bounteous Progress. The love interest is subordinate and often loosely linked with the main theme, but the heroine's crossed fortunes in love may provide an excuse for the plot and a means of rewarding the winner; and in general it is youth that wins, not by desert, but by wit and cunning. Plays such as *Your Five Gallants* and *A Mad World* are vivid enough to transport us to a still living world, but one which is narrow and often unsavoury, the society it represents being one bent on material advantage. An audience as money-conscious as the characters in the play would expect the graspers to be outwitted as a matter of course, yet as the decade draws on Middleton's work for the theatre begins to recall not only the content of his early satires but their moral viewpoint, and their light-hearted irony begins to combine with a cautionary tone which would not be out of place in the popular tract. The three plays which form the subject of this chapter, though all in line with Middleton's characteristic citizen comedy, are of particular interest in that their developing moral attitude points forward to the greater work of his later years, and though all three are written to a basically conventional pattern, they catch the interest of a modern reader just where they seem to depart from it.

There is nothing original in the plot of *A Trick to Catch the Old One*. In order to extract money and the forfeited mortgage on his lands from his parsimonious uncle, Lucre, Witgood stages a familiar confidence trick, passing off his mistress, a courtesan, as a rich widow whom, he gives out, he is about to marry. In fact he is in love with Joyce, niece of old Hoard, but secretly, since Hoard is his uncle's inveterate enemy. Thus Middleton provides himself both with a conventional means of tying up the plot and an excuse for keeping an unwanted heroine out of the action, for Joyce appears only once before the end of the play.

Dazzled by his nephew's prospects, Lucre is ready to give him all he desires, but the 'trick' has an additional twist in the rivalry between Lucre and old Hoard, both old and miserly and therefore good stage subjects for gullery. The spectacle of old Hoard falling easily into the trap and all but forcing the courtesan into marriage with himself to spite his enemy, of the two old rogues outdoing one another in malice to gain possession of Witgood's cast-off mistress and incidentally relieving his financial embarass-ments, is one of the most delicious pieces of fun in the drama of the period. The double intrigue provides an unflagging variety of incident, meticulously balanced so that the three groups in-volved and their domestic background—the Lucre and Hoard households and Witgood's lodgings with his circle of assistants and creditors—are continually before our attention. These are typical figures, yet we come to know them as individuals and to enjoy their company.

A Chaste Maid in Cheapside, though not next in date, follows a not dissimilar pattern. Again the intrigue is between the young and the old, again the love interest forms the immediate excuse for the plot, again a courtesan is passed off as a coveted match. But whereas Witgood's chosen bride is of so little importance that we almost forget her existence, Moll Yellowhammer, endowed with the romantic aura of the distressed damsel, is placed, like Witgood's courtesan, at the centre of the intrigue. Moll is the victim of the avaricious schemes of her parents, Yellowhammer the rich goldsmith and his wife Maudlin. A good deal of the action centres round the efforts of her lover, young Touchwood,

to free her from their grasp and from the power of Sir Walter
Whorehound, a dissolute knight whom, for his social pretensions,
the snobbish citizen and his wife fancy as a son-in-law. But both
suitors have other connections important to the plot. Sir Walter
has two mistresses; one is a Welsh courtesan whom (following
Witgood's ruse) he passes off as a rich heiress to 'some nineteen
mountains', and disposes of in marriage to Tim Yellowhammer,
son of the goldsmith and a student at Cambridge; the other is
Mrs. Allwit, whose husband complacently permits the knight
to beget his children in return for keeping up the house. Allwit
is the 'king of Wittols', his wife the 'great whore of spittals'.
On the other hand, Touchwood has an elder brother who is in
trouble because he cannot support the children it is his fatal
proclivity to beget in and out of wedlock; but he makes a little
money—and provides a good deal of incidental amusement—in
offering his services to the bemused Sir Oliver Kix, on whose lack
of offspring depends Sir Walter's possession of his lands.

Middleton's skill in thus combining one section of the plot with
another and making rich comedy out of every link, however im-
probable, distinguishes this play amongst other citizen comedies
of the period. The variety of incident, the speed with which
episode succeeds episode so that no character is out of view for
long, in what might have been a difficult story to follow, sustains
a reader's interest and must have been effective in the theatre.
Familiar as the pattern may be, there is not a dull moment, and
the background is etched in with the vividness and precision
characteristic by this date of Middleton's work.

All this amoral trickery, barely compensated for by the
marriages by virtue of which both courtesans forswear their past
life while the true lovers are united, is typical of Middleton's
comedies of this period. The Widow[2] however, though conceived
on conventional lines, differs from them in that the plot is less
dependent upon intrigue than upon character under the influence
of circumstances.

Francisco has designs upon Philippa, the young wife of
Brandino, an elderly and doting Justice. Philippa, only too happy
to be won, suggests an assignation in a faked letter, purporting
to come from himself, which she conveys to him under the pretence of returning it in righteous indignation. Francisco is quick
to take the hint, but he has involved himself in his friend Ricardo's

scheme to entrap into marriage yet another of Middleton's desirable widows, Valeria, sister to Brandino, in this case a genuine prize, by causing her to make a seeming avowal before concealed witnesses. But Valeria is too quick for him, and Francisco is arrested along with Ricardo. Both young men are bailed however —Ricardo by the quixotic second suitor to Valeria, who in his truculent old man's fashion suddenly conceives a 'humorous' affection for him, and Francisco by Brandino, whom he has persuaded to regard himself as the preserver, not the seducer, of his wife's honour. Both young schemers thus owe their freedom to the fallibility of old age.

At this juncture Middleton introduces the thieves, an entertaining trio of comedians, Jacobean Marx brothers, equally at home as freebooters or quack doctors. With his customary carelessness of the unimportant detail that might clog the action, Middleton summarises in Francisco's own comments the latter's further misfortunes at their hands.

It is at this point that a new element enters the plot. Now benighted and hopelessly delayed, Francisco is disturbed by the figure, lurking in the shadows outside Brandino's house, of Martia, in flight from a despotic father and an unwelcome match, whom the thieves have also waylaid and have stripped of her man's disguise down to her shirt. Believing he sees his father's ghost Francisco is conscience-stricken. Thenceforward providence, rather than human ingenuity, shapes the action to thwart the frivolous and the lustful. Philippa and her attendant Violetta are foiled by their own trick, for Francisco falls in love in earnest with Martia whom, in revenge for his defection, they present to him in woman's dress on the assumption that she is a man disguised as a woman. Meanwhile Ricardo who, for all his recklessness is sound at heart, is rewarded with the hand of his widow to the chagrin of her covetous suitors. In fact the light-hearted comedy develops a recognisably moral tone in the closing scenes of the play. It is the better nature of Francisco and Ricardo, not the compulsion of circumstances alone, that brings them to a resolution; it is thus that fate or some influence outside the witty intrigue takes charge of the honest, and the not-so-honest are discountenanced.

The recurrent pattern however persists and while, as suggested above, something may be due to Middleton's familiarity with classical comedy, these stereotyped groups of characters and the intrigue in which they engage have a traditional interest possibly deriving from the scenarios of the old Commedia dell'Arte. Whether they consciously recognised them or not, many in Middleton's audience might recall these interludes of improvised acting, familiar at fairs and on public holidays, and still more their equally familiar stock characters—the predatory Punchinello, the aged and foolish Pantalone, the adroit Arlecchino (Harlequin), younger, quicker to gain advantage; then the secondary characters, the pedantic doctor or physician, the rascally serving-man, Scapino, the pert waiting-woman, Columbine—the types are ageless and so are many of the masks they wore and the jokes they cracked. Few modern playgoers remember the Commedia dell'Arte, but the crowds which throng round the seaside Punch and Judy shows which derive from them are not all composed of children! This feeling for tradition is an element to be reckoned with in Middleton's plays. His recurrent plots are in the convention and so is much of his characterisation. For instance the disguised courtesan posing as a bride, the disguised thieves doing business as quack doctors,[3] the disguises by which the young lovers, often the hub of the intrigue in the scenarios, outwit their obdurate elders are all familiar and all in the popular tradition.

Whether created thus consciously or unconsciously, Middleton's Lucre, Hoard and Witgood in *A Trick* reproduce the triangle of Punchinello, Pantalone and Arlecchino—the old schemer, the old gull and the clever trickster—while the Host, who acts as serving-man and go-between for Witgood, in association with the Courtesan, is not unlike Scapino with Columbine. These conventional characters, either singly or in association, playing similarly typical roles, reappear continually in Middleton's comedies; the middle-aged grasper—Quomodo of *Michaelmas Term*; Yellowhammer of *A Chaste Maid*; the foolish old man—Sir Oliver Kix in the latter play, Sir Bounteous Progress of *A Mad World*; the relatively unimportant lovers, Maria and Geraldine of *The Family of Love*, Moll and her Touchwood of *A Chaste Maid*. Ingenious men-servants, pert waiting women, gullible old men, disguised courtesans and distressed damsels persist even into Middleton's later work. Whatever their precise ancestry they never repeat themselves, indeed the freshness with which Middleton can conceive his personages within a well-worn convention is a facet of his achievement, and if the fun sometimes takes a sinister turn it owes much of its effect to the familiarity of the associations it suggests.

For while the type remains the comedies show an increasing interest in individual idiosyncrasies as a hallmark of character. This is especially true of the three plays in question; whether satirical or farcical in approach the chief characters are conceived, if not in the round at least as recognisable human beings with a recognisable background. Lucre and Hoard of *A Trick*, for instance, are built up with meticulous care and though alike in greed, as personalities their rivalry in villainy enriches them both. Stage villains, even in farce, are generally designed to arouse dislike as well as laughter; here the trickster's own foibles are engaging enough to claim attention irrespective of their deserts. Lucre is clearly drawn as the self-made man of substance, delighting in having about him men of discretion and dispatch—such as he believes his nephew's messenger to be—despising and not scrupling to exploit the failures and the luckless. It is automatic that when his nephew's fortunes apparently take a turn for the better, he should see in him, not only a means to his own advancement, but also an excuse to triumph over first his enemy, then his second wife and her blockhead son. His private reflections pinpoint the man.

> Good heaven, who would have thought it would ever have come to this pass! yet he's a proper gentleman i'faith give him his due, marry, that's his mortgage: but that I ne'er mean to give him: I'll make him rich enough in words, if that be good; and if it come to a piece of money, I will not greatly stick for't.
> [II.1.177]

Indeed Lucre will stick at nothing. His own method of securing a rich widow is to seduce her while time and opportunity serve, so as to 'make all safe' before marriage. Hoard's less prudent expedient is to abduct her and marry her in haste; but it is the guilelessness of these hardened schemers that seems to interest their creator. Impelled by jealousy and avarice, they are eventually caught in their own toils and there is something near pathos when Lucre, driven to playing the kind uncle in handing over the mortgage which he had determined never to relinquish, appeals

in a sort of desperation to those better instincts in Witgood, which
his whole behaviour has hitherto discounted:

LUCRE:	You must conceive it aright, nephew, now;
	To do you good I am content to do this.
WITGOOD:	I know it, sir.
LUCRE:	But your own conscience can tell you I had it
	Dearly enough of you.
WITGOOD:	Ay, that's most certain.
LUCRE:	Much money laid out, beside many a journey
	To fetch the rent; I hope you'll think on't
	nephew.
WITGOOD:	I were worse than a beast else, i'faith.
LUCRE:	Although to blind the widow and the world,
	I out of policy do't, yet there's a conscience,
	nephew.

[IV.2.47]

For the moment Lucre seems to talk himself into a belief in his
own pose of self-sacrifice; meanwhile it is Witgood's turn to play
deliberately upon the streak of simplicity in his worldly-wise
uncle which for Middleton is the chink in every man's armour.

Hoard, like Lucre, is bemused in a dream of wealth that never
comes true Nevertheless the dream is worth enjoying while it
lasts—so agreeable indeed, that he is all but charmed out of his
own avarice. 'Wilt thou never be thankful?', he exhorts himself,
'how dost thou think to be blest another time?'. Hoard has a fine
relish for the appurtenances of dignified substance.

> . . . the journey will be all, in truth, into the country; to ride
> to her lands, in state and order following; my brother and
> other worshipful gentlemen . . . to ride along with us in their
> goodly decorum beards, their broad velvet cassocks, and chains
> of gold, twice or thrice double.

Malvolio's dream of greatness was not more circumstantial. And
with what unctuous pleasure, in his new role of country squire,
he summons his newly appointed household about him:

> I promise you my masters, I take such a good liking to you
> all; I put you already into my countenance, and you shall be
> shortly in my livery . . . But you my falconer and huntsman, the

welcomest men alive, i'faith ... Go you knaves all, and wash
your lungs i'th'buttery, go.

[IV.4.10 and 49]

It is the typical small townsman's dream of expansive country
housekeeping.

With his newly wedded wife, Hoard is almost uxorious; even to
call her by his own name is to savour the sense of possession:

> Wife, Mistress Jane Hoard ... I would but know sweet wife
> which would stand best to thy liking, to have the wedding din-
> ner kept here or i'th'country ... Hoard bear thy head aloft,
> thou'st a wife will advance it.

[IV.4.80]

When we see him again, he is a host on a generous scale—a con-
noisseur of wines, fastidious as to his 'cupboard of plate set out',
in love with his liveries, 'every time I think on 'em', jesting
gallantly on his unfurnish'd house' and what he takes for the
bashfulness of his bride—above all, feasting his enemy. For Lucre
is there to look on and, Hoard trusts, to envy. We live through the
dream with him as, for the duration of a scene, we live through
Malvolio's dream, but when disillusionment comes in this shrewd
castigation of the money-loving citizen, there are no sympathetic
major characters to distract attenion from his disgrace. But satirical as its overt purpose may be, the play remains on the level of
light comedy, and the whole dilemma resolves itself in terms of a
double Elizabethan pun: Hoard has married a 'Dutch widow',
and Witgood, in subsequently marrying Hoard's niece, has
acquired, both in the real and the slang sense, an 'aunt'.

The delineation of the characters in *A Chaste Maid*, though no
less convincing as realistic portraiture, has a tartness which will
be considered later. But *The Widow* is a new departure in itself;
for while the play seems to be designed for a large cast of boy
actors, with a wide range of characters, the general tone is
markedly different from that of *Your Five Gallants* and *A Mad
World*, or even from that of *A Trick* and *A Chaste Maid*. The
light-hearted episode in which Ricardo and Francisco demonstrate for one another's benefit the way to woo a widow, is human
as well as entertaining. The two friends are sharply differentiated
—Ricardo the lucky, ingenious adventurer, whom the fates

favour for his innate goodness of heart, Francisco the serious, romantic lover, doomed to mischance by his ill-timed susceptibility to the appeal of both friend and mistress. This is gay where *A Trick* is satirical. The characters here are fundamentally moral even if superficially aslant, and we accept them as credible transcripts from life. Philippa and Violetta are exceptions but they are outwitted in the end, while the thieves and the suitors are background figures whose main function is relief. In Lucre and Hoard, though neither character remains at the level of caricature, the greed of old age and its absurdity are simultaneously exposed; but there is no vice in Brandino's stupidity and we laugh with him, not at him. Middleton is more interested in his foibles than in his faults, and his partnership with Martino, whose doglike devotion extends even to an aching tooth in sympathy with his master's sore eyes, creates a master and man relationship which reconciles us to them both. Among Middleton's early comedies, this play is an interesting exception.

Although it may be fairly safe to discount the supposed collaboration of Fletcher in this play, some instances of unwonted romanticism or deliberate sententiousness may well derive from Fletcher's influence. The runaway Martia, her disguise as a man, the pathos of her distressed condition, the passion which she arouses in another woman and finally her own love at first sight for Francisco and their subsequent union, albeit in line with the conventional romantic tradition, are after the manner of Fletcher and are new to Middleton. So also is the conscious deliberation, again new to Middleton at this date, with which Francisco, believing he sees his father's ghost communes with his conscience and from a would-be seducer of another man's wife, becomes a repentant moralist. His father's memory—we have already heard a good deal about Francisco's father—his duty to an old family friend, the warning of Providence which has so far prevented the fulfilment of his illicit purpose, weigh upon his mind, and after a day of irresponsible behaviour like the prodigal son he comes to himself. This repentance, not from sheer pressure of circumstances as is usual even in Middleton's most serious plays, but from the realisation of a better nature in a new or unwonted situation, is characteristic of Fletcher.[4] Yet Middleton perhaps thought the incident important enough to recall in the latter part of the play, for Francisco seems to refer to it in his advice—

'Heaven will not let you sin and you'd be careful' (V.1.424). This
may be of little importance in itself; it is an approach to character
familiar enough in later Elizabethan and Jacobean drama, in a
good deal of which Fletcher's influence must be recognised. It
does however betoken in Middleton's own outlook an interest in
the romantic or self-analytical character which made possible such
tragic conceptions as we shall find in *Women Beware Women*.
Whether deliberately or not, Middleton seems increasingly to be
departing from the presentation of a type, however functional or
entertaining, towards a conception of comedy broader than that
contained in anything he had written before *A Trick to Catch
the Old One*.

The realism of this world of tricksters is more than that of a
faithful record. In *A Trick to Catch the Old One* the world is
also frankly one of merriment, yet there is a distinct contrast
between the presentation of Lucre and the probably earlier sketch
of an elderly middle-class go-getter deceived by a shrewd young
kinsman in *A Mad World my Masters*. Sir Bounteous Progress,
landed gentleman of ostentatious means, is a caricature of pretentiousness, existing only to be exposed, and the exposure is good
fun as well as good theatre. But across the light-hearted comedy
of *A Trick* there sometimes falls a shadow. It is Witgood himself
who warns us not to take the situation as mere matter for amusement.

> He has no conscience, faith, would laugh at them;
> They laugh at one another.
>
> [IV.2.85]

Beneath the castigation of middle-class over-reaching in quest of
social status we may glimpse a human capacity for self-betrayal.
Looked at through Witgood's eyes the entire play is equivocal.
Witgood's claim to be contracted to a widow is true in the
obverse, the slang meaning of the word; the Courtesan's modest-
seeming assurance that she has 'nothing' is true in a sense that
Hoard does not dream of; Lucre's hoped-for triumph over his
enemy and his wife in his nephew's match, is substantiated only
in that he sees Hoard confounded by succeeding where he himself
has failed; in the event it is Witgood who gains the sole advantage,
and when Hoard invites Lucre to his wedding dinner, it is to
witness not his good fortune but his shame. 'The world is so

deceitful', says the Courtesan as she carries her own deception of
Hoard to its climax. The ludicrousness of the situation lies in that,
astute as they are by nature, the characters nevertheless rush into
it with unconsidered haste. It is an ambivalence that goes deeper
than the double connotation of Elizabethan bawdry; the humour
has an edge, a twist, that anticipates the tragic irony of Middleton's later plays and which we hear in the metallic tone of the
Courtesan's defence upon discovery:

> Despise me, publish me, I am your wife;
> What shame can I have now but you'll have part?
> If in disgrace you share, I sought not you . . .
>
> [V.2.134]

> If error were committed 'twas by you;
> Thank your own folly.
>
> [V.2.143]

For the moment we have reached the limit of satirical comedy.

This inherent seriousness emerges as the plot develops. It
remains a question whether the comic reversal of Lucre's purposes
or the Courtesan's struggle for reinstatement is the real centre of
interest in the later scenes of the play. True the strife between
uncle and nephew and the determination of either to exploit the
other's weakness or misfortune, is a dominant theme, while Hoard
is a mere pawn in Witgood's game. But the Courtesan is more
than this. The undemanding frankness with which she accepts
her position is disarming, and easy as her morals may be, we are
bound to credit her avowal that she is true to Witgood's 'follies'.
She is, moreover, the one person in the play who shows compunction. She recognises a debt of affection to Witgood—who returns
it only perfunctorily—and she is remorseful when the latter's
appeal to her to induce Hoard to defray his debts conflicts with
her new loyalty as Hoard's wife.

> But methinks, i'faith, you might have made some shift to
> discharge this yourself, having in the mortgage, and never have
> burdened my conscience with it.
>
> [IV.4.182]

There is also some emphasis upon her genuine desire to do well.
Witgood asserts that 'She never had common use nor common

thought' (V.2.133), and her own promise to amend must be taken
seriously:

> Though I have sinn'd, yet could I become new,
> For where I once vow I am ever true.
>
> [IV.4.149]

This is in the vein of *The Honest Whore* and *The Roaring Girl*,
the type of play which Middleton wrote in early years only in
collaboration with Dekker, and to which he returned in *Women
Beware Women* where Bianca lays claim to a similar right to
regeneration. The Courtesan's final rhymed speech of repentance
may be mere stage convention, yet even here she is no lay figure;
her development from whore to respectable wife is delicately
handled and on the whole convincing. In fact the theme of
rehabilitation becomes insistent during the closing scenes of the
play.

Middleton may enjoy the spectacle of villainy, especially
when he can set one rogue to undo another, and he never shows
us the repentant sinner in a state of grace,[5] yet his sympathy with
the outcast's desire for reinstatement prompts him to provide a
consoling finale even at the expense of a good joke. For instance
in *A Chaste Maid* when Tim is similarly tricked into marriage
with a courtesan, his mother's tart remark:

> You told me once by logic you would prove
> A whore an honest woman; prove her so Tim,
> And take her for thy labour.
>
> [V.4.95]

would have neatly rung down the curtain on this caricature of
academic pedantry, but Middleton cannot leave it there. The
courtesan reminds him that 'There's a thing called marriage and
that makes me honest', and the play leaves this strange couple
setting forth into problematic respectability like Hoard and his
bride in the earlier work.

Considering the satirical tone of these citizen comedies, written
immediately for the Children, the stress laid upon the stabilising
effect of marriage is worth noting. When, after the frivolous
gaiety of the last Act of *The Widow*, Philippa takes revenge upon
the defaulting Francisco by throwing in his way the attraction of
what she believes is a man disguised as a woman, his audience

would no doubt have thought it enough to have the tables thus
turned for the fun of it; for Francisco falls in love with Martia
and Philippa's mischief-making reverts upon herself in the loss of
both objects of her fancy.[6] But the play ends surprisingly with a
joint sermon by the rebel daughter and the would-be seducer on
the value of honest wedlock and rearing a family.

MARTIA: Be good.
FRANCISCO: Be honest.
MARTIA: Heaven will not let you sin an you'd be careful.
FRANCISCO: What means it sends to help you, think and
                    mend.
MARTIA: Marry you speedily;
                    Children tame you, you'll die like a beast else.
                                                                        [V.1.423]

In *A Chaste Maid* Middleton seems to go out of his way to
develop the same theme when Touchwood senior, having temporarily denied himself his wife's company to check their fruitful-
ness, outlines the ideal of married state:

                              A man's happy
     When he's at poorest, that has match'd his soul
     As rightly as his body . . .
     Had her desires been wanton they'd been blameless
     In being lawful ever; but of all creatures
     I hold that wife a most unmatched treasure
     That can unto her fortunes fix her pleasure
     And not unto her blood: this is like wedlock;
     The feast of marriage is not lust but love
     And care of the estate.[7]
                                                                        [II.1.23]

     Unpleasant as is the world depicted in *A Chaste Maid in
Cheapside*, marriage and child-getting, the importance of building up a family and substance, are dominant interests. Granted
that the attitude to these matters is equivocal, yet Allwit, the willing cuckold, and Yellowhammer, the avaricious citizen, are significant here because they constitute a denial of just these things
—a denial which is refuted in the end. In the code of both, greed
excuses lechery; barrenness follows as a natural consequence. Allwit's house is, nevertheless, much blessed with children whom he

delights in as if they were his own, poor Touchwood senior is over-blest and so is the country girl whom he has seduced; meanwhile, after quarrels and reconciliations, the loving but barren couple, Sir Oliver and Lady Kix, produce, by what means Sir Oliver is too simple or too happy to enquire, the child whose birth unstates the arch-villain Sir Walter Whorehound. The announcement, 'Sir Oliver Kix's wife is new quickened', marks the climax of broad comedy in the under-plot, and is designed to produce a laugh; at the same time, falling as it does in the midst of the tension created by Whorehound's belated repentance and revulsion from his former associates, it has the effect of positive relief. With this news Sir Walter ceases to be of consequence; Allwit must henceforth get his own children and, since the knight is no longer a covetable match, Moll may be free to marry as she pleases.

Against this broadening conception of life Middleton's careful depiction of a realistic background has a dimensional importance. In contrast to such satirical comedies as Jonson's *Epicœne* or his own *Your Five Gallants* the background to the characters in these three plays seems to emanate from themselves, just as in actuality knowledge of a man's environment stamps his neighbours' conception of him. Middleton has a gift for seizing on the pivotal detail which brings a locality to life, with the life of the people who move within it. For instance we know that Lucre's house abuts upon the street, for Hoard intends to 'pass by his door of purpose . . . and have our horses curvet before the window'. We know of the hall in Hoard's house where his new livery men wait to be hired, and of the garden, though we do not enter it, where his bride entertains her guests. Even the accommodation at the inn is carefully detailed as part of the characters' situation;—the gentlemen are shown upstairs into the 'Pomegranate' while the other party rest downstairs 'in this little room'. There is a similar particularity in Francisco's survey of Brandino's house in the opening scene of *The Widow*—'the prettiest contriv'd building this'—with the posy under 'the great brass squirt' and the upper windows which overlook Brandino's office. It is a fair impression of a typical 17th Century interior and it also, incidentally, uses the upper and lower stage levels which we shall meet again in *Women Beware Women*.

In *A Chaste Maid in Cheapside* the background is even more

lavishly imagined. Allwit's house is described in sufficient detail
for us to plan its extent; there is the coalhouse with 'five or six
chaldron new laid up', the back yard where you will 'find a
steeple Made up with Kentish faggots, which o'erlooks The
waterhouse and the windmills', the hall where Alwit receives his
patron, the courtyard before the house where the ladies of the
Sisterhood dispute precedence on entering as to the christening
feast, and above all, Mrs. Allwit's bedchamber, with the fair
needlework stools for the gossips, the displaced floor rushes, the
nurse's dish of sweetmeats and—merging character into background—the tasselled handkerchiefs spread in the greedy laps
ready to pocket them. Allwit's comments on the furnishings in
their disarray stamp the man as well as his environment:

> Look how they have laid them,
> E'en as they lie themselves with their heels up!
> How they have shuffled up the rushes too, Davy,
> With their short figging little shittle cock heels!
> These women can let nothing stand as they find it.
>
> [II.2.187]

Allwit's house is as much a part of himself as it is of the theme of
domesticity abused in which he plays a major role.

It is clear that for Middleton character and environment are
interdependent, yet interiors have for him a fascination in themselves. House interiors are elaborated by being given access to
clearly located streets and gardens, rooms open into other rooms
or on to galleries. Middleton is always nervously aware of life
being lived, not only between the people on the stage, but also
beyond the confines of the scene he portrays. The effect is both
to strengthen the impression of the characters as real people in the
complexity of daily life and to reconcile us in some measure to
their follies. Middleton's sense of background lends a certain
dignity, a solidarity, to figures which might otherwise degenerate
into Aunt Sallies. Without the environment which informs them
Lucre and Hoard could have flattened into grotesques. Life may
be cruel and degrading as we see it in *A Chaste Maid* but it is still
life. Chastity is rare in Cheapside, but it is Cheapside represented
by Allwit and the Yellowhammers, not chastity in the persecuted
Moll, that motivates the plot. The spectacle of one cuckold fond-
ling the bastard children reared in his own house, of the other

lighting bonfires to celebrate the consequence of his wife's seduction, of the Sisterhood mingling drunken piety with fatuous chatter at the christening of Sir Walter's unacknowledged child, has an acrid irony softened by the irresponsible merriment which the background realism, integral to the theme of this play, enables the audience to share. In *A Trick to Catch the Old One* laughter is cut short by a cautionary hint from the stage. In *A Chaste Maid* laughter is encouraged as much by familiarising the audience with the play world as by the sheer audacity of the characters' behaviour, but the more we laugh the more sharply we experience the significance of what is happening. It is this duality of vision, this harmonising of the comic with the near tragic within a familiar context, that makes for the uniqueness of this play. It is also the first clear indication of qualities which would later distinguish Middleton's contribution to tragedy.

The constant presence of Allwit gives the mockery a deeper significance. Allwit's contribution to the comedy lies in his capacity for survival in face of those who despise him and are despised by him. Amongst the greed or lust driven, he is distinguished by his cool common sense, his instinct for the prudent thing to do in every kind of emergency. But the character has ironic significances already built up by his association with Davy Dahanna, his fellow parasite and Sir Walter's poor kinsman. Like Davy, Allwit is a detached observer, and this detachment from the ordinary human standpoint invests him with an incisiveness unusual even in Middleton at this time, and anticipating the conception of De Flores in *The Changeling*. The same detachment places Whorehound, who for all his villainy has some rudiments of conscience, entirely in his power, and when, realising in time that Sir Walter has outlived his usefulness, he turns him out of doors, the real nature of their association is sharply clarified.

SIR WALTER: If ever eyes be open these were they.
Gamesters farewell, I've nothing left to play.
ALLWIT: And therefore get you gone, sir.
[V.1.149]

Having had the last word, Allwit is left to gloat over his ill-gotten gains.

Sir Walter's first appearance in Allwit's house is the meeting of

two rogues, each contemptuous of the other, each oblivious to the
other's opinion. Sir Walter's lordly entrance and Allwit's obsequious welcome are balanced by the latter's shrewd asides:

> SIR W.:   Slippers! Heart you are sleepy.
> ALLWIT: The game begins already. (Aside)
> SIR W.:   Push, put on Jack.
> ALLWIT: Now I must do't, or he'll be as angry now,
>   As if I had put it on at first bidding;
>   'Tis but observing,
>   'Tis but observing a man's humour once,
>   And he may ha' him by the nose all his life. (Aside)
>   [I.2.73]

On the knight's threat of marriage however, it is Sir Walter's turn
to 'observe':

>   That wakes the slave
>   And keeps his flesh in awe. (Aside)
>   [I.2.98]

whereupon Allwit once more savours his power over the man who
disdains him:

>   I'll stop that gap
>   Where'er I find it open: I have poison'd
>   His hopes in marriage already with
>   Some old rich widows and some landed virgins . . .
>   He's yet too sweet to part from.
>   [I.2.99]

Here, more even than in Middleton's earlier artificial comedy,
the sardonic nature of the situation depends upon the audience's
participation in it. Allwit makes a similar appeal to the audience
in his running commentary on the gossips at the christening feast:

>   Now out comes all the tasselled handkerchers,
>   They're spread abroad between their knees already;
>   Now in goes the long fingers . . .
>   [III.2.51]

>   These women have no conscience at sweetmeats
>   Where'er they come; see an they've not cull'd out
>   All the long plums too.
>   [III.2.62]

This vigorous detail which brings the scene to life, also underlines the collapse of Puritan respectability with which the christening began. As good cheer begins to do its work, Allwit continues:

> Now the cups troll about
> To wet the gossips' whistles; it pours down, i'faith . . .
> Now bless thee, two at once! I'll stay no longer
>
> [III.2.77]

and he has his final thrust at the Sisterhood as he watches their departure:

> Go take a nap with some of the brethren, go,
> And rise up a well-edified, boldified sister.
>
> [III.2.178]

Though as yet only on the level of comedy, Allwit's comments have the destructive significance of Famineo's thinly veiled gibes as he watches his sister's quarrel and reconciliation with her lover in Webster's *The White Devil*. It is worth noting that *Middleton* uses this method of commentary largely in scenes in which Allwit appears.[8] Being unmoved by moral sanctions, Allwit is immune from opinion, and from the fear of social ostracism that dogs other characters—the Yellowhammers for instance—whose remnants of conscience occasionally inhibit their natural vitality, and possessed of a clarity of vision that detaches him even from his own actions. Twice we find him analysing himself; first in the unctuous self-congratulation with which, on his first appearance, he contrasts his own masterpiece of opportunism in willing cuckoldry with the 'night-piece' of other less astute and more conscience-burdened men; secondly when, in disguise and with equal relish, he comments on his own complacent cuckoldry to Yellowhammer:

> Knows? ay and glad he may too, 'tis his living;
> As other trades thrive, butchers by selling flesh
> Poulters by vending conies or the like, coz.
>
> [IV.1.225]

The humour in this episode anticipates the self-delineation of the chief characters in *A Game at Chess* but its purpose is of course quite different. Like De Flores, whom he resembles on the comic

level, like Webster's Flamineo in his self-congratulatory remarks
to the audience, Allwit is an artist in low living, and his dramatic
significance is the greater in that he is simultaneously comic and
satanic, a combination of some importance in Jacobean tragedy
as Webster understood it.

It is in the scene of Sir Walter's repentance that this dual
quality emerges. A sustained attention seems to have gone to the
making of this episode. The knight is borne in wounded and
apparently dying; the context is traditional and Sir Walter is
presented as the typical deathbed penitent exhibiting a pious
revulsion from his former evil life. At first the three parasites
surround him to voice the conventional forms of grief, but every
lachrymose phrase from Allwit's mouth has its derisive under-
current.

> What shall become of us! . . .
> This is no world for me whene'er he goes;
> I must e'en truss up all and after him Davy;
> A sheet with two knots and away.
>
> [V.1.1]

The jigging rhythm of the last line suggests the complacent leer
given verbal expression at the end of the scene, where the assumed
sorrow of 'What shall become of us!' devolves into:

> What shall we do now wife . . .
> We're richly furnish'd wife,
> With household stuff.
>
> [V.1.156]

It is in the context of domestic comedy that Allwit becomes 'the
principal agent of retribution',[9] his ministrations to the dying
man barely concealing his malice. His insistence on 'knowing'
recurs like a refined torture:

> . . . he knows me not
> Call me to mind; is your remembrance left?
> Look in my face; who am I, an't like your worship? . . .
> He will begin to know me by little and little
>
> [V.1.15]

Significantly the same idea recurs in the wounded man's own
words,

> Thou knowst me to be wicked . . .
> None knew the dear account my soul stood charg'd with
> So well as thou.
>
> [V.1.24]

and appropriately Allwit now becomes for him more malignant
than a devil:

> No devil can be like thee! . . .
> . . . like hell's flattering angel,
> Wouldst never tell me on't, lettst me go on . . .
>
> [V.1.22]

Irony deepens when Allwit calls upon his wife who, he says,
was 'wont to do good to him', and his victim's misery is
heightened to breaking point when, in accordance with the pro-
prieties of the deathbed, the children, the living evidence of his
lechery, are brought to him. It would be interesting to have the
prompter's notes at the knight's cry, 'Wretched, death of seven!'
Evidently seven children are introduced, and with some emphasis
for, since there is no previous enumeration of Sir Walter's
children, we are plainly meant to attach particular significance
to the number here. Sir Walter evidently sees his seven bastard
children as embodiments of the seven deadly sins come to dog
him at his end; if we take this piece of stage business seriously,
we must do so in terms of the morality tradition.

It is with the same fundamental significance that the wounded
man shrinks from Allwit's proximity—'my wound aches at thee'
—recalling the superstition that the wounds of the victim will
bleed in the presence of his slayer, for Allwit is also 'poison' to
his heart. But the knight's will, anxiously prompted by Allwit, in
which he bequeaths to the latter a legacy of curses, concluding
with a wretched death, is directly in line with folk tradition.

> What will you give to your brother John?
> A gallows tree to hang him on.
>
> [Border Ballad]

This is a recurring theme in the ballads, and it creates here an
interlude in which even the irrepressible Allwit is momentarily
shaken.

This sympathy, almost instinctive, with folk feeling and primitive tradition may be caught here and there throughout Middleton's dramatic writing.[10] But it is never more deliberately enunciated than here, where he seems at pains to give full value to both levels of significance, the comic and the near tragic, on which the scene is built. Sir Walter is allowed more volubility than are most of Middleton's characters when at the point of death; his sense of inward suffocation recalls, Claudius' frustrated attempt to pray under Hamlet's observation.

> Who sees me now,—O and those so near me
> May rightly say I am o'ergrown with sin.
> O, how my offences wrestle with my repentance!
> It hath scarce breath;
> Still my adulterous guilt hovers aloft,
> And with her black wings beats down all my prayers
> Ere they be half-way up. What's he knows now
> How long I have to live? O what comes then?
>
> [V.1.71]

But it is in the child that the horror of the situation receives that additional twist characteristic of Middleton; Nick, pushed forward to speak to him, replies with an eloquent simplicity:

> I dare not, I'm afraid.
>
> [V.1.39]

With the news of Touchwood's death there follows a dramatic change of tone when Allwit reveals himself for what he is:[11]

> Let the law lift you now that must have all;
> I have done lifting on you, and my wife too.
>
> [V.1.112]

Throwing off his deception, Allwit assumes, dressed in the remains of Whorehound's bounty, the new part, which he will probably play for the rest of his life—that of a prosperous and therefore ostentatiously law-abiding citizen:

> I'll harbour no such persons as men-slayers
>
> [V.1.115]

> I pray depart sirs,
> And take your murderer along with you;
> Good he were apprehended e'er he go,
> 'Has killed some honest gentleman
>
> [V.1.138]
>
> I must tell you sir,
> You have been somewhat bolder in my house
> Than I could well like of.
>
> [V.1.142]

And the balance of comedy is pleasantly restored in Mrs. Allwit's reply to the appeal of her discarded lover:

> Alas, sir, I am one that would have all well,
> But must obey my husband.
>
> [V.1.129]

In thus conducting the dialogue on two contrasting levels however, Middleton had achieved a deeper analysis of feeling than the scope of comedy allowed; impressive as it is the scene suffers from this departure from light satire. Sir Walter's utterances are commonplace compared with those of the comic figures, Allwit and his wife, and it is possible that Middleton, never an imitator by nature, was deliberately trying to please a popular taste by experimenting—and to some degree fumbling—with the methods of revenge tragedy.

Again the diabolic streak in Allwit is in keeping with the peculiarly mordant nature of this play. Even the hardened rogues of *A Trick* overstep themselves; Lucre is blinded by his own greed, Hoard by fabulous dreams of his own triumph. In *The Widow* pardonable recklessness, a sort of 'humorousness' in the satisfying of human sensibility, is dominant—in Ricardo's thoughtless trick to win Valeria, in Brandino's readiness to be hoodwinked in deference to his old friend's memory—even in the Second Suitor's partiality for Ricardo which costs him his pretensions to Valeria's hand. In contrast Allwit takes no risks; there is no fringe of mixed motive to his purposes, no reconciling fallibility. Yellowhammer alone is his equal and Allwit's ruse to prevent the marriage between Moll Yellowhammer and Whorehound temporarily fails only because the goldsmith is as ruthless as he. Yet human foibles, which call for exposure rather than attack, are a better basis for comedy as such, than wickedness.

Comedy is concerned with the immediate and familiar, the transitory and the odd, but the diabolic character carries us into universals which are not easily reconciled with the commonplace. It is some evidence of Middleton's control of his material that he can use such a character, not to dominate but to throw into sharp relief, the social types with which he is surrounded.

There is a certain inevitability in Allwit's meeting with Yellowhammer. Middleton's treatment of the citizen and his family has a savagery which would have wrecked the play, were it not balanced by the gently farcical studies of Touchwood Senior and Sir Oliver Kix and his lady. From the opening scene where we find Maudlin bullying the love-sick Moll, Yellowhammer and his wife have no redeeming feature. Maudlin's silly pretensions to social grace, Yellowhammer's determination to amass wealth whatever the means, their joint pride in their ludicrous son, 'the Cambridge boy'—this citizen snobbishness is typical of a social class which touches the lesser nobility on the one side and the learned professions on the other. Maudlin's attempts to construe, her pleasure in gossiping with Tim's tutor, and Yellowhammer's jovial impatience with her, are pleasant touches of realistic comedy. Yet while this presentation of the goldsmith and his family poses the follies of a rising middle class as matter for laughter on the one hand, it produces them as evidence of downright viciousness on the other. Yellowhammer's determination to exploit his own children is paralleled by physical cruelty in the comparatively simple Maudlin—the unvarying stupidity of the wives of Middleton's villains is worth noting—dragging her runaway daughter by the hair, 'not like a mother'. His own persistence is as ruthless as shrewd:

> The knight is rich, he shall be my son-in-law;
> No matter, so the whore he keeps be wholesome,
>
> [IV.1.258]

is his comment after Allwit's disclosure about Sir Walter's private life. His reaction to Moll's serious illness and to the news of Touchwood's death, following his own unkindness, is solely to make a new plan:

> . . . now wife, let's but get the girl
> Upon her legs again, and to church roundly with her;
>
> [V.2.78]

and when he believes her dead and all his expense upon her
'cast away', he is visited by no more grievous feeling than the
typical citizen's apprehension of what the neighbours will think:

> All the whole street will hate us and the world
> Point me out cruel.
>
> [V.2.94]

Still more typical is his determination, in spite of all reverses,
to have his son married to the 'rich Brecknock gentlewoman', to
which Maudlin replies with characteristic predatoriness:

> Mass, a match;
> We'll not lose all at once, somewhat we'll catch.
>
> [V.2.100]

This exposure of baseness under the citizen's respectable flat
cap is amusingly parodied in Tim's preoccupation with his sister's
epitaph:

TIM :   Faith busy, mother, about an epitaph
             Upon my sister's death.
MAUDLIN :   Death? She's not dead I hope?
TIM :   No, but she means to be, and that's as good . . .
             Looks she like death, and ne'er a word made yet?
             I must go beat my brains against a bed-post
             And get before my tutor.

> [V.2.8]

Such deliberate violence to the sensibility might find its place in
the plays of Wycherley or Congreve, whose work Middleton
often seems to foreshadow; here however it serves to restore the
balance. We may feel disgust for Yellowhammer and his wife,
but we can do no other than laugh at Tim.

To make merry at the expense of human pretentiousness, even
if positive values suffered in consequence, was part of Middleton's
purpose in the citizen comedy of this period. Yet for Middleton
silliness was never far removed from moral turpitude, and
although he was too good an artist to be obtrusively moralist, a
definite, albeit negative system of ethics emerges. Cruelty and
avarice are near allied and neither is amusing in itself. The

tenacity of Witgood's creditors and the rapaciousness of the
lawyer Dampit, like the cupidity of the Yellowhammers, are
etched with a repulsiveness which implies a moral intention. It is
the more significant that it is a minor character who comments
on the lawyer's exactions and on his fate as the mark and conse-
quent doom of all parasites:

> LAMPREY: Note but the misery of this usuring slave:...
> Here may a usurer behold his end: what profits it to be a
> slave in this world, and a devil i'th'next?
>
> [*A Trick*, IV.5.58]

According to Sir Philip Sidney in his *Apologie for Poetrie*, it is
the property of comedy to represent 'the common errors of our
life . . . in the most ridiculous and scornful sort that may be;
so that it is impossible that any beholder can be content to be
such a one.' No doubt many among Middleton's audience would
have piously endorsed this view, and some of his early comedies,
like those of Ben Jonson, conform to it. But we cannot find the
predatory characters in *A Chaste Maid in Cheapside* merely
ridiculous—they are far too clever; we do find them dangerous
and unpleasant. Nor are his comic conceptions, for the most
part, merely amusing. There is little to suggest that Middleton
liked his characters, or that liking had much to do with his choice
or handling of them. Yet the fascination which the kaleidoscope
of human behaviour had for him was in itself an objective
sympathy, a kind of *agape*, which enabled him to examine them
nearly and accurately, but always in action and in association
with one another. For Middleton the average human being—
and his human beings were always average—had no meaning in
isolation. It was the friction of similar types, not the tensions of
the unique personality, that caught his interest. If he believed
in the existence of the unique, it was not his business to portray
it, and Middleton was essentially a writer who knew his business.
So in *A Chaste Maid* Allwit survives and Yellowhammer manages
pretty well; the comedy is saved by the brilliance of its patterning.
It is part of the quality of this play that there is no attempt to
disguise or extenuate, but we are moving away from light comedy
as such.

In these comedies Middleton works with a surprisingly small
number of themes, but with a seemingly inexhaustible number of

variations on those themes. His skill is less in inventing plots than in so constructing the play as to distil the maximum incident and amusement out of them. In *A Trick*, Witgood's suggestion that the Courtesan shall also provide for herself stems from his own trick upon Lucre, but the disposal of the two angles of the plot so that the rivals, Lucre and Hoard, may deceive one another, and in so doing replenish Witgood's purse, is a piece of ingenuity both balancing the pattern of the play and underlining the whole situation with a rich irony. We often meet greedy tricksters and false brides in Jacobean drama, but few so cleverly placed in relation to one another as these. In *A Chaste Maid* the careful balancing of the dilemma in the Touchwood household against the frustrated hope of issue in Sir Oliver and Lady Kix, turns a situation which would in any case be highly entertaining into uproarious farce. Even in *The Widow*, more popularly and less incisively conceived, the contrast in nature between Ricardo and Francisco is underlined in Ricardo's demonstration of successful wooing, and resolved when in the final Act both gallants achieve a true marriage by methods conforming to their respective types. Similarly Valeria, abhorring falsehood and seeking a true mate, is set against her sister-in-law, the restless and well named Philippa,[12] and the Second Suitor's irascible affection for Ricardo is coloured by Brandino's pathetic faith in Francisco. Again the situation in Allwit's house is highlighted in the story, parallel in fact though dissimilar in tone, of Sir Oliver and Lady Kix. It is this habit of providing the additional touch, the 'turn of the screw',[13] that distinguishes Middleton's comic irony in these plays. They are still good reading, still very actable and with an audience more witty than squeamish they could hardly fail to please.

Middleton's technical skill and richness of invention are sufficient to compensate for occasional discrepancies in the plays as they now stand. If Hoard's plot to secure the widow should fail, Sam Freedom and his mother, Lucre's second wife, are ready with another. Yet after this evidence of a possible rift in the Lucre household has fulfilled its function in building up his character, we hear no more of their plans.[14] The kindly maid Susan—evidently she was at some stage important enough to bear a name—appears from nowhere to aid the denouement of *A Chaste Maid*.[15] Something has been forgotten in revision or

deliberately abandoned. Similarly a good deal of the action in
The Widow is left to the imagination. But in every example what
is important is the unerring judgment that determines the kind
of omission which will pass unnoticed. Middleton knew better
than to lengthen the action merely in order to forestall questions
which his audience might never ask.

Pattern, the juxtaposition of character, the balance of comparable situations—these are dominant elements in Middleton's
plays of this period. If this work written largely for the Children's
Companies in the private theatre, gave him the opportunity he
needed to turn his natural gifts of observation to a dramatic use,
it also taught him that reticence and selection which were to
remain with him as a habitual discipline. Yet during these years,
the shaping of a situation as part of an intrigue, which he had
brought to a fine pitch of artistry in such comedies as *A Trick to
Catch the Old One*, was increasingly enriched by a study of
human personality under the pressure of circumstances which
we have seen developing most clearly in *The Widow*.

All this seems to reach a climax in *A Chaste Maid in Cheapside*, the play which most clearly represents what Middleton had
built upon his experience in comedy written primarily for the private theatre, and which with its technical skill in handling both
character and theme, seems to look forward to the later tragedies.
It may well be true that Middleton might never have been the
artist he ultimately became without this preliminary training in
sophisticated comedy.

So far he had found his strength in exploring the equivocal
nature of a basically comic situation, composed of an incongruous
set of circumstances and the absolute unreason of ordinary men
and women—with the stress on 'ordinary'—and he would bring
it to full fruition in his later plays. We shall find no tragic greatness among the characters of these plays, not because he found
greatness inadmissible, but because he could not find it relevant
to what he had to say about the human condition as he saw it.
Middleton's basic scepticism, never devolving into cynicism, ad-
mitted a belief in the consistency of human character which he
never relinquished to achieve an emotional or artistic effect. This
is the consistency which he had laughed at in Hoard and
Brandino, gently derided in Valeria's Second Suitor, and defined
in Allwit, Yellowhammer, Maudlin and Tim as Jonson defined

his humours. The problem of reconciling this human idiosyncrasy with the deeper complexities of character and behaviour had yet to be faced. It was in the company of an artist as dissimilar to himself as Rowley that he tried to solve it in *A Fair Quarrel*.

3. A Transitional Play: *A Fair Quarrel*

IT is easy to overlook the importance of Middleton's collaboration with Rowley when involved in the thankless task of assigning authorship. The extent of Rowley's contribution, whether it was on an equal footing or whether Rowley merely revised Middleton's work,[1] is a small matter beside the profound changes in the two plays which Middleton wrote after 1613 while Rowley was his partner. Hitherto Middleton's plays had depended largely upon intrigue in which character and action had developed through combinations of circumstances; the situation dominated the play. Now in *A Fair Quarrel*, and later on in *The Changeling* —and for that matter in the two last plays following—the action turns rather upon human intercourse, the rub of one character upon another, upon the variety and clash of temperament among people bound by ties of sympathy or some emotional involvement. Whereas dramatic interest had centred on brief satirical episodes in which author and audience shared information hidden from the characters, now the tendency is towards the longer developed scene built up on a variety of pace and planes of feeling. In this process *A Fair Quarrel* marks a point of transition in which the authors seem to be gathering their resources before turning to tragedy in *The Changeling*.

Middleton had made good use of Jonson's lead in the comedy of the 'humours' over the years in which he had written for the Children; now he had to find his own way in a theatre comparatively new to him, a theatre in which the influence of Fletcher was dominant. No one who hoped to work for the popular theatre could ignore the challenge of Fletcher. Evidence of his influence in *The Widow* has been noted; in *A Fair Quarrel* Middleton seems to reassess that challenge before passing on to his mature and independent work. No doubt it was under the same influence that the main plot of *A Fair Quarrel* was conceived; on the other hand the sub-plot follows the familiar pattern of domestic intrigue, so that the play is an interesting combination of new and older elements. Though by no means a perfect play, to some extent it is a sample of the dramatic methods which Middleton was to use with distinction in later work.

The play opens with a long expository scene in Russell's house, the main location of the sub-plot but also the place where both sides of the action meet. Russell we immediately recognise as the typical avaricious father to whom a marriageable daughter is a valuable commodity. He plans to match his daughter Jane to money in the person of Chough, a simple but wealthy Cornish heir. But Jane is already pre-contracted to her lover Fitzallen, whom Russell pretends to encourage but plans to remove by having him arrested for debt at his own family gathering. One of the first arrivals is Russell's sister Lady Ager whose fatal weakness —an anxious devotion to her son, Captain Ager—manifests itself at once in a rush of tears at the news that Ager and his friend the Colonel are returning from service and will shortly join them. When the two young men and their friends arrive the Colonel, an older soldier than Ager, raises furious objections to being compared with his friend in valour and a quarrel ensues.

Immediately the contrast between the two men, a contrast of character which is to motivate the main plot, emerges. Whereas the Colonel is hasty and fiery tempered Ager has a cool reasonableness which neither detracts from his own merit nor insults the dignity of his temperamental friend, but which nevertheless adds fuel to the fire. It is Russell who intervenes—and we sense his authority as he does so—by prudently persuading them both to yield their swords. Meantime we learn that Jane is with child by Fitzallen, so that when Russell's plot matures and, at a signal, the officers enter to arrest him, Jane's plight becomes serious. But Fitzallen is a kinsman of the Colonel who flies to his defence—impotently without his sword—and when Ager tries to calm him, turns upon his friend with the accusation —'Thou'rt the son of a whore'. A challenge follows and the scene closes with the lovers' agitated farewells.

Admittedly the scene has its longueurs but it is an excellent piece of exposition, probably also an unusually good example of well-knit collaboration.[2] Middleton was to recall its skill and its variety in later plays. More important is the development here of the economy of the opening scene in *A Chaste Maid in*

Cheapside. Here as there the scene selects what is necessary to
the plot, less in circumstance than in those aspects of character
in Lady Ager, Ager and the Colonel, and in Russell himself,
which will determine their behaviour later. From this point,
embroidering nothing, Middleton allows the characters in both
plots to follow the bent suggested here, as the play sweeps to its
climax.

As Ager approaches his home the reflective side of his nature
asserts itself. Being slow to anger Ager will not fight unless he
is assured of the justice of his cause; personal honour cannot be
served if Honour itself is violated. He loves and honours his
mother, yet the Colonel is his friend and suppose the accusation
is true?—then to fight would be a mortal sin. Here for the first
time, I believe, a character in Middleton expresses that devotion
to an abstraction which Fletcher was developing as a dramatic
theme and which would be of importance in the coming Stuart
drama.

After the first shock when Ager puts her to the test, Lady Ager's
sole thought is for her son's safety. Taking advantage of his
scruples she makes him believe the slander is a fact. To the bewilderment of his supporters Ager then refuses to fight and instead
makes a moving appeal to the Colonel to abjure violence, whereupon the latter, sheathing his sword, accuses Ager of cowardice.
Now this is the opportunity Ager looked for, this charge he *knows*
is false. A fierce combat ensues and the Colonel falls, apparently
fatally wounded. When, again in deep dejection, Ager returns
home Lady Ager admits the truth, that she is and always has been
an honest woman, and mother and son are joyously reunited.

Now this situation is no less artificial than that in *The Maid's
Tragedy* in which Amintor is torn between personal honour and
loyalty to the King who has betrayed him into marriage with his
mistress as a screen for his own lust, or that of Maximus in
Valentinian (probably entirely Fletcher's work), equally confused
by claims of fealty to the Emperor who has raped and thereby
caused the death of his wife Lucina. Superficially the solution in
the main plot whereby the Colonel, repenting on what he believes
is his deathbed, leaves to Ager all his possessions including the
hand of his sister, is in keeping—a suitable marriage for a young
man already wedded to an idea! But Middleton relieves the story
of its unreality first by the immediate build-up of an unusually

convincing relationship of mother and son, and then by the
delicate humour with which the whole web of romantic nonsense
is treated.

Lady Ager's reaction to her son's doubts is that of any woman
of spirit; she first strikes him and then reminds him sharply of
what he knows—her own virtuous life and constant widowhood.
Ager's joy is characteristic—it is 'the joyfull'st blow that flesh
e'er felt'. But this is no satisfaction to his mother. Her pride is up
—'honour doubted is honour deeply wounded'—but her anger is
tempered with the good sense he and his rash friend so clearly lack.

> This is no question to be slighted off,
> And at your pleasure closed up fair again,
> As though you'd never touched it.
>
> [II.1.187]

Lady Ager's plain statements have a curiously modern touch.
It is only when she realises that something more than family
honour—her son's safety—is at risk that her mother's affection,
no less impulsive than his idealism, reasserts itself. ''Las I shall
lose him'—she begins to play a part and she plays it badly.

This protracted revelation of something fabricated is a device
which Middleton will use to more sinister effect in tragedy.[3] The
hint, the reiterated 'you must not go' (to the duel), the anguished
plea 'faith, do not know And yet obey my will', the half statement of something more significant than his present cause—
'one that makes this nothing'—the painful reference to 'that
secret That will offend you' and a last appeal to him not to
press her—'I dare not . . . I dare not: 'Twas your own seeking
this'—these are the fumbling hesitations of a forthright nature
violating itself. As the dialogue continues Ager's distress emerges
as something far deeper than the scruples of a hypersensitive
conscience such as we find in Fletcher. For Ager absolute honour
is more than a figment of chivalry, it is identified with absolute
truth. His mother who once embodied that truth is now false, a
discovery beyond moral sentiment. This is sheer reversal, the
unthinkable which nevertheless must be thought.

> If you mean evilly,
> I cannot understand you; nor for all the riches
> This life has, would I.
>
> [II.1.174]

This emphatic simplicity, with the falling monosyllables, aptly expresses the shocked bewilderment of the natural truth-teller struggling to face reality.

In what follows the word 'false' recurs like an obsession: 'That you were ever false . . . False! . . . False! do not say't for honour's goodness do not You never could be so . . . O, were you so unhappy to be false.' The same word punctuates Ager's reactions in their next meeting when Lady Ager declares the truth: 'Why were you never false? . . . Not false at all? . . . I kneel to a woman that was never false.' But when at the urging of his friends Ager goes to the duel, the collapse of her subterfuge seems to her the judgment of truth itself:

> . . . truth's angry with me
> In that I would abuse her sacred whiteness.
>
> [III.3.23]

Finally for Ager himself when he has the best of the fight in 'a fair quarrel'—'Truth never fails her servant'. It is this burning conviction that honour is truth and will admit no compromise and that conventional valour is an emptiness beside it that sets Ager and his mother apart from the other characters, a distinction which Lady Ager acknowledges with a touch of irony:

> My passion is not every woman's sorrow;
> She must be truly honest knows my grief.
>
> [III.3.41]

The effect of the scene on the field is to place Ager's moral predicament under the cool scrutiny of the outside world. His modest tribute to his friend's quality, his plea for tolerance as opposed to violence, simply bewilder his opponents as well as his supporters. It is Ager, not the Colonel, who is on trial; what he says he means sincerely and even the Colonel admits that it is well said, but it is the wrong time to say it!

Now this incongruousness is of the essence of comedy. As the Colonel sheathes his sword we know that Ager is the better man, but the Colonel is the wiser and when on being accused of cowardice Ager falls to the attack with boyish glee, the point is underlined in the half sardonic comments of his friends. To make fun of the conventional duellist had been popular in the theatre since Shakespeare turned Mercutio's irony upon the valiant—

and humourless—Tybalt in *Romeo and Juliet*. Now a similar douche of cold water is turned upon Ager's belated display of valour:

> 1st. Fr.: An absolute punto, hey?
> 2nd. Fr.: 'Twas a passado, sir.
> 1st. Fr.: Why let is pass an 'twas, I'm sure 'twas somewhat. What's that now?
> 2nd. Fr.: That's a punto.
>
> [III.1.156]

Though he does not know it, Ager's exhortations are being applied to himself; the more correct his behaviour the more ludicrous he appears.

The scene of Ager's second homecoming is a gentle parody of the first. It is built to a similar pattern but every parallel with the first episode is heightened to the verge of comedy. As before Lady Ager enters full of motherly anxiety, but whereas previously her purpose was a courteous request that he would not leave England again, now she comes to call for a surgeon before even discovering whether her son is hurt. As before, the truth as she tells it dawns slowly upon Ager; as before the word 'false' is three times repeated, but this time the mounting tension of discovery, his abandonment to love and worship of the woman who now is both 'dear' and 'good', accelerate to a crest of naïve enthusiasm which is to carry him to yet another combat. The whole episode is informed with a lovable absurdity on which Lady Ager's lines are a shrewd comment:

> What an unhappiness have I in goodness!
> 'Tis ever my desire to intend well
> But have no fortunate way in't.
>
> [IV.3.84]

The comedy of good intentions could hardly go farther, but we have come a long way from the satire of Middleton's citizen plays. We are also in a world totally different from that of Fletcher. Whether Ager's convictions are tenable in a real situation or not is of little consequence. What matters is that the whole character is involved both in the loftiness of his idealism and in the comedy that arises from it. Lady Ager admits that her 'wretched affection' is the cause of all the trouble, but we do

not doubt the reality of her love because it manifests itself in
tears and excessive maternal care. In contrast to the central
figures of Fletcherian tragi-comedy Middleton's characters are
often most moving when most absurd.

Against this scrutiny of an idea and its expression in human
conduct the development of Jane Russell's story is a supporting
theme. Jane is saved from the attentions of her unwelcome suitor
by her condition, which her father takes to be indisposition. The
marriage contract is signed but Jane is placed in the care of the
Physician and his sister Anne. In his house her child is born and
afterwards the Physician promises to protect her reputation provided she will yield to his lust; when she refuses he threatens to
'spoil' her marriage. Now this, of course, is precisely what Jane
wishes and the tyrannical father falls into the trap. Believing
that the Physician is the father of her child he willingly pays
Fitzallen's debts in order to get his daughter married—so once
more a trick is played 'to catch the old one'. It is now Fitzallen's
turn to demand his price; having secured an addition to Jane's
dowry, the lovers reveal the truth and the wedding dinner prepared for Jane's marriage to the still heart-whole Chough serves
to celebrate their own union. Meanwhile the Colonel, now re-
covered, is reconciled to his friend and Ager is united to his sister;
so the play ends with the inconsequential happiness of comedy.

Setting aside Jane's anticipation of marriage,[4] her resistance
to the Physician's advances, in which she has the moral support
of Anne his sister, is a reflection of Ager's devotion to integrity;
in the sudden acceleration of tension in their relationship the real
strength of her position is obscured and she seems to represent
beleaguered chastity as the persecuted 'chaste maid', Moll
Yellowhammer, does not.

There is a certain similarity in manner between the scene
(III.2) in which the Physician tempts Jane and that in which
Lady Ager deceives her son. Taking advantage of her courteous
enquiry as to how she may requite his kindness the Physician
tries to trap her with that verbal play which Middleton will use
to more sinister effect in the tragedies. He begins by deliberately
confusing her with the double connotation of the word 'love';
she can render 'love for love' . . . 'You have confess'd My love
to you'. When the point is pressed, like Ager she is merely bewildered—'I understand you not'—and the leer in his reply—

'Fie you do'—is enough to indicate her danger. Like Ager, Jane takes refuge in incredulity until he resorts to a second pun— 'Indeed I love you . . . What deed?—The deed that you have done'. But it is his falseness rather than his lechery that makes him 'the outside of a man', a 'false man', and to Jane as to Ager, falseness is the basis of evil. Different as is the context of these two episodes, Jane's reactions, from confusion, through bewilderment and disbelief to shocked realisation, are precisely those of Ager to his mother's deception. The scene in the sub-plot underlines the meaning of that in the main plot—the impression of innocence sorely tried.[5]

But there is another facet to the kind of falseness Jane encounters in the Physician. The Physician is a born equivocator, all his methods are roundabout, and the less effective because they are based on conventional and therefore in this case fallacious assumptions. At their first meeting when he tries to diagnose her trouble, Jane's forthrightness exposes the tortuousness in himself:

> Lord, what plain questions you make problems of!
> Your art is such a regular highway,
> That put you out of it and you are lost.
>
> [II.2.22]

It is only after much verbal fencing[6] in which the high-spirited patient outdoes him at his own subtlety, that he can triumphantly affirm the obvious—'Now I have found you out; you are in love'.

In the temptation scene her shock of realisation, after the apparent good will she has experienced from him, is underlined by the comedy inherent in the same false assumptions. Women who fall from virtue are fair game; it is easy to ensnare an unskilled girl by wit; women in Jane's predicament will pay any price to obtain the security of marriage. Twice she tries to break through his circumlocutions with a straight question—'Is this the practice of your physic-college? . . . I asked it before,—Is it a practice among you physicians?' (III.2), from which his sole refuge is professional mystery:

> Tush, that's a secret; we cast all waters:
> Should I reveal you would mistrust my counsel.
>
> [III.2.114]

In the end it is his love of intrigue that preserves her both from himself and from a false marriage. Having 'fished with silver hooks and golden baits' the Physician is caught in his own cunning. Perhaps the incomprehensible verbiage of the other medical man in the play, the surgeon who attends the Colonel, has some bearing here. Having vainly tried to find her way through the learned entanglements with which he answers her anxious question as to her brother's health, the Colonel's sister comments:

> What thankless pains doth the tongue often take
> To make the whole man most ridiculous!
>
> [IV.2.35]

Before the plain simplicity of truth the jargon of the learned, the conventions of the soldier's code, the cleverness of the schemer, are all 'ridiculous'.

It is worth remembering that one reason for the popularity of this play in its time was the 'roaring' which centred round Chough and his man Trimtram. So popular were these characters —another example of the master and man relationship which Middleton had used so pleasantly in *The Widow*—and their activities in the roaring school, that an additional scene of 'roaring' (IV.4) was included, according to Bullen, 'when the unsold copies were reissued with a fresh title page!'[7] Chough and his always half sceptical follower and dependant Trimtram, are good fun as they anxiously follow with writing tablets the instructions of the usher in the roaring school, and even to a modern reader these scenes with their fertility in verbal monsters are still racy. There is an element of comic relief here in the quarrel that rages among the students of roaring (IV.1), for the rule is that 'there must be wine ready to make all friends, for that's the end of roaring'. This quarrel is 'valiant but harmless', and the easy-going Chough likes it the better 'because no blood comes on it'. Perhaps to a contemporary audience the light-hearted Chough and his valiant companions were all the more comic for their implied comment on the sophistications of the serious characters on both sides of the plot.

Nevertheless the over-emphasis on the roaring interest in the version of the play that has come down to us contributes to its imbalance. The main and secondary plots with the ancillary roaring scenes are too dissimilar to dovetail. It is true that superficially the two plots in *The Changeling* differ no less, but in that play the Governor's castle in the main plot and the school for fools and madmen in the sub-plot serve as ironic counterparts so that the one enriches the other. Here the sole link is the mechanical one of kinship and the family circle and neither theme is sufficiently developed to make an entity in itself. If as seems possible, the authors were each basically responsible for a section of the play, each subsequently revising the other's work, the lack of an over-all unity is understandable. But in intention the play does cohere and the intention probably proceeds from the mind of one author.

Middleton had already shown signs of Fletcher's influence in his handling of Francisco's troubled conscience in *The Widow*; here the major theme is built on lines which would not be out of place in any Fletcher play. It is the series of anticlimaxes, increasingly comic, each with its implied comment on what has gone before, that makes of it an assessment rather than an imitation of what Fletcher had done with his partner Beaumont in tragedy, and was about to produce alone after Beaumont's death, in tragedy and tragi-comedy. It is difficult to resist the conclusion that the particular impact of this play comes from Middleton's critical but fair-minded scrutiny of a new mode in the theatre in which he was establishing himself.

The mechanics of the play are totally—perhaps in the main plot intentionally—unreal. Considering the care with which the characters of Lady Ager and the two contestants are sketched in the opening scene it is odd that we are expected to accept as credible a man who will make such a charge against a woman—and that the mother of his close friend—whom we are given no reason to believe is anything but above reproach. It is equally strange that Russell, who is at least no fool, should not immediately connect Jane's child with the lover he has taken such pains to remove. If Middleton was mainly responsible for the play he evidently thought that neither the sententiousness of the main plot nor the familiar domestic intrigue of the supporting story would lose anything in being presented as much ado about nothing.

The importance of this play is in its fresh approach to fashionable and well-tried dramatic themes. After the mordant satire of *A Chaste Maid in Cheapside* the gentle irony of this play is a surprising new development. Even the intriguers do so little damage

that we cannot take their malice very seriously. Yet conflict there
is and it goes to the roots of character and behaviour. It is not the
fashionable notions of honour or valour that are exposed for what
they are worth, but the pretentiousness of human aspirations.
Ager's devotion to truth finds its realisation not in his own
attempt to define the absolute but in the natural truthfulness of
his plain forthright mother. The arrogance of the Surgeon and
the wit of the Physician are silenced not in the reversals of the
play's denouement but by the good sense of Anne and the
Colonel's sister, as well as by Jane's unspoilt sincerity, which
makes the counter-intrigue possible. The sophistication on trial
in this play is seen as a matter of morals as well as of manners.
Middleton has turned from social satire to pursue the consistency
of character he had observed as a human characteristic in the
citizen comedies to a level at which a code of conduct as well as
a whole personality, is at issue.

From their several ordeals the main characters emerge unsul-
lied because they are pure in heart. The two tragedies which followed after about 1620 would be concerned with the not so pure
in heart. It was the character torn by the mixed motives, the
naïve aspirations, the self-evasions of common humanity that
would inspire Middleton's dispassionate analysis of conduct and
situation in *The Changeling* and *Women Beware Women*. But
it was here in this hybrid play, and probably with a good deal of
practical help from Rowley, that he first evolved a dramatic
situation from the psychological tensions within the characters,
tensions which could evoke compassion and laughter simultaneously. The discovery here that a near tragic situation can be
most moving when it trembles on the edge of absurdity led to the
still more important discovery that a lightweight character can
be capable of tragic experience. In this sense *A Fair Quarrel*
marked a transition from satirical comedy to a new kind of drama
based on tragi-comic irony in which, in his own time, no one
could follow him.

A Fair Quarrel was perhaps the climax of Middleton's association with Rowley. Whatever the latter's share in it Middleton
returned so often to the manner and content of this play that it is
difficult to believe he was not the major partner. Lady Ager's
hesitant build-up of the deception she practises upon Ager is
recalled in the psychologically unerring scene in which Livia

betrays Isabella to incest in *Women Beware Women*; the Physician's temptation of Jane is echoed, stage for stage, and here and there verbally, in the more carefully developed scene in *The Changeling* where De Flores compels Beatrice to face the consequences of her new relationship with himself after[8] the murder of Alonso. Temptation scenes evidently had a fascination for Middleton and he was to return to a similar pattern of protracted communication in a play as dissimilar as *A Game at Chess*, where the Black Bishop's Pawn tries to corrupt the White Queen's Pawn much as the Physician tries to seduce Jane. The use of the pun, of verbal play, of the careful placing and repetition of the significant word which he employs in this play were to be important devices in his mature work. In all this *A Fair Quarrel* is a first study for much of Middleton's later achievement.

More significant in regard to subsequent work is the theme which informs the play—the opposition of truth and feigning. Hitherto patterns of action, the recurrent intrigue, had been the preoccupation in Middleton's plays, but a theme which could in any sense be termed moral had never been more than slightly suggested. The theme enunciated in *A Fair Quarrel* is developed further in the tragedies—in the challenge of fact to fantasy in *The Changeling*, of integrity to compromise in *Women Beware Women* and of self-knowledge to self-evasion in both plays. Significantly when Middleton returns to satire in *A Game at Chess* the whole play turns upon a conflict between truth and falsehood, sharply defined both in the political allegory of the Black and White Houses and in the situation of the White Queen's Pawn. This is a surprising development in a dramatist hitherto so little given to didacticism.

Whether or not a 'message' was any part of Middleton's conscious intention, he was beginning to formulate a view of human behaviour which would be basic to his later plays. After *A Fair Quarrel* the issues he presented to his audiences would never be simple, but he would never again subscribe to a mode or follow a lead. His return to the popular theatre and the demands of a wider audience had opened up for him a fresh approach to drama, and one in which he could be master. He had used and reassessed a contemporary trend in *A Fair Quarrel*; a year or two later, still with Rowley's co-operation, he was to attempt a revival and reshaping of the pattern of Elizabethan Revenge tragedy.

4. *The Changeling*

> I am that of your blood was taken from you
> For your better health.

WITH this wry joke the heroine of *The Changeling* sums up as she dies her relationship with her father and her assessment of herself—yet another authoritative father and yet another rebellious daughter. But rebellion is no longer romantic or justifiable, nor does it bring anything other than disillusionment either to Beatrice, the heroine, or to De Flores her agent, whose repulsiveness, setting aside his cleverness, proves to be her most dangerous temptation. We have come a long way from Moll Yellowhammer and the runaway Martia and these vestiges of the traditional pattern only emphasise a profound difference in outlook. Traces of Webster's influence in earlier plays have already been touched upon and we shall find in *The Changeling* similarities to Webster's tragedies which cannot be ignored, but Middleton himself was probably scarcely aware how individual was the venture when with Rowley he turned to tragedy in, or about, 1621.

Many of his contemporaries would have seen in the story on which *The Changeling* is based a plot for a conventional drama of revenge. But Middleton was following a natural bent in finding in it the experience of a group of quite ordinary people whose fate is the logical consequence of their obtuseness and simplicity. Had any of the characters reached what Webster would have recognised as tragic proportions the balance and the significance of the play would have foundered. For here the keynote is mediocrity, a mediocrity which Middleton had learned to transmute into poetry, and the action turns upon the contrast between the characters' demands upon life and their limitations when an unwonted set of circumstances reveals them. Now this is the basis of comedy, and Middleton was undoubtedly taking risks with his audience in using the methods and attitudes, even at times the situations, of comedy to produce the effects of tragedy. The play, like *Women Beware Women* which came later, has unquestioned

50

moral implications, but its ironic overtones are those of *A Chaste Maid*. The action reaches the tragic level through the acuteness of that psychological insight which Middleton had developed in his middle comedies, but we see the characters moving to their destruction less as the victims of their passions, than of their capacity for evasion and self-delusion.

The problem of what the eyes see as opposed to what we think they see is set in the forefront of *The Changeling* when Beatrice warns Alsemero on hearing that he loves her:

> Our eyes are sentinels unto our judgments,
> And should give certain judgment what they see;
> But they are rash sometimes, and tell us wonders
> Of common things, which when our judgments find,
> They then can check the eyes and call them blind.
>
> [I.1.74]

This is a summary of Beatrice's own predicament; throughout the play illusion and reality press their claims upon her until they finally destroy her, but not until she has plumbed unexpected recesses in her own nature and in the nature of other characters associated with her.[1]

The basis of the plot is a story from Reynolds' *God's Revenges Against Murder* of 1621. Beatrice Joanna, daughter of Vermandero, Governor of Valentia, is driven to instigate the murder of the suitor of her father's choice, Alonso Piracqo, in order to wed her new lover, Alsemero. She employs as her agent a member of her father's household, De Flores, a not unattractive young man who aids her without ulterior motive. Thereafter she has to reckon with her problematic relations with her husband while this secret lies between them, but she is a faithful and devoted wife until his unaccountably jealous temper drives her for solace to her former accomplice. A liaison follows. The pair are overheard and betrayed by a waiting woman, whereupon the girl confesses to murder in the cause of love in the hope that her husband will not probe further to discover her adultery with De Flores. But Alsemero demands the whole truth and, in anger, destroys them both. Later he meets his own death on the scaffold for killing (in a duel) Alonso's brother Tomaso.

Such is Reynolds' story in outline.[2] Middleton preserved the names of the original characters, but it was the web of motive, not the intrigue itself, that caught his eye and his modifications are significant. The original Beatrice meets Alsemero, the lover of her choice, before being betrothed to Alonso. In the play Beatrice and Alsemero fall in love at first sight, only seven days before the date arranged for her wedding with Alonso; moreover some emphasis is laid on Alonso's simple faith in his prospective bride's affection, despite the misgivings of his brother Tomaso. Thus a straightforward conflict of wills is transformed into a moral issue. This Beatrice is at grips, not with her father's wishes only, but with moral and legal sanctions. She may get her own way, but she can never be in the right; she is 'a whore in her affection'.

Again, the original De Flores laid no claim to Beatrice until she herself turned to him for comfort; Middleton defines the situation by making him repulsive to the audience and abhorrent to the heroine, and possessed with a ferocity of purpose which sticks at nothing until he has her in his power. Thus Beatrice's action is not only a bid for freedom, it is also a dangerous gamble. The irrational jealousy of Reynolds's Alsemero becomes an uncompromising uprightness, which drives her into the yet more dangerous subterfuge of bribing her waiting woman Diaphanta to take her place on the nuptial night.[3] When Diaphanta fails to return from the bridal chamber as the dawn breaks, Beatrice consents to De Flores' expedient to rouse and then destroy the waiting woman by setting fire to her room; but the device is dramatically effective, not merely as a further step in Beatrice's downfall, but as an additional link with the man who in agreeing to act as her tool has become her master.

In the play events are telescoped so that the discovery and the violent deaths of Beatrice and De Flores (not at Alsemero's hands but at those of De Flores himself) occur within twenty-four hours of the wedding night; meanwhile Tomaso presses his demand for the truth about his brother's death, not upon Alsemero primarily, but upon Vermandero, and he is carefully kept out of the way until the discovery is ripe. All this has the effect of preserving the integrity of Alsemero's character, while it also shapes the dramatic significance of Tomaso who haunts the wedding festivities like an embodiment of justice, as Alonso's ghost haunts his murderers. Reynolds' story has the mechanical quality of the traditional vendetta, but Middleton's Beatrice is no Vittoria Accorambona, though their stories are not dissimilar; nor on the other hand has she the stoicism of Hardy's Tess, who, like her, is played upon by her husband's ideal of honour. She is a frightened girl unable to control the forces that her self-will has unleashed. It is with characteristic irony that Middleton focuses the play not as in the original story, or as Fletcher would have done, on Alsemero's reactions as the just man betrayed,[4] but on the dilemma of Beatrice whose means to freedom becomes the cause of her enslavement, so that she encounters the moral justice she has flouted in the husband she had hoped to enjoy.

Beatrice acts without forethought or compunction. In the ill luck of her premature betrothal she clutches at a chance hint in conversation with Alsemero; De Flores is always 'i'th'way' and fit for foul uses. It will be very clever to use the object of her hate to make accessible the object of her love, and she will be free—from her importunate suitor and also from his 'dog-face'. The phrase is significant: De Flores is the dog-face of fact, the hard features of reality, and Beatrice in following her fancy has reckoned without reality.

This is the crux of the problem and the setting of the plot contributes to it. Beatrice is presented like a princess in a fairy tale, only child of a kindly and influential father, with an eager suitor, a secret lover, a useful confidante and, withal, a waiting gentleman who adores her from his inferior station; Beatrice is the conventional fortunate child, set amidst the stage properties of romance. Even the less pleasant elements of the story—the strange closet with its half magical potions with which Alsemero tries to test her chastity, and the substitute bride on the wedding night —are all part of the charming fairy tale in which later De Flores supplies the role of ogre. Step by step this dream world is unbuilt, and Beatrice herself, shorn little by little of her adolescent naïvety, is brought ever closer to the man she abhors and the reality that he embodies.

The climax is, however, meticulously prepared for in the episode (II.2) in which Beatrice incites De Flores to the murder of Alonso. The skill in double asides, which Middleton had practised in citizen comedy, is utilised here, as Webster frequently uses it, to build up the tragic theme in the minds of the audience. Beatrice plunges into her project, De Flores listens greedily, each oblivious to the other's reactions. His implied assurance of payment on his own terms—'That I've thought on . . . the thought

ravishes'—passes her by, but it sufficiently defines her position;
meantime her own reflection—'I shall rid myself of two inveterate
loathings at one time'—is a neat rejoinder to his dream: 'Me-
thinks I feel her in mine arms already' (II.2.144, 149). It is in
the characters' failure to communicate that we have the clearest
forecast of their destruction, while De Flores' observation that
'Some women are odd feeders' (II.2.153) suggests the mutual
miscalculation which their next meeting will confirm.

Middleton evidently spent a great deal of care on the scene
in which De Flores claims his reward (III.4). As we have seen, his
mastery of protracted discovery had its first clear promise in the
Physician's attempt upon Jane Russell in *A Fair Quarrel* (II.1),
and there are similarities here which suggest that he was consciously recalling that episode.[5] Parting from her lover Beatrice
meets De Flores in a glow of pleasant expectation, in the 'reful-
gent virtue' of her love. The irony of the phrase we discern
instantly when De Flores exclaims on his own side: 'my thoughts
are at a banquet', relishing in advance the 'sweet recompense'
(III.4.18 ff). Still oblivious to her own guilt Beatrice weeps for
joy, when upon this happy irresponsibility there impinges the first
challenge of reality, the physical ugliness of murder, in the dead
man's finger with her own ring upon it which De Flores presently
produces.

If Middleton's audience was familiar with the incident in *The
Duchess of Malfi* in which Ferdinand presents the Duchess with
a dead man's hand, this gesture might appear an appropriate
opening for De Flores' attack, for it carries the same sinister
associations, the same effect of shocking the victim into temporary
inactivity.[6] At the same time its violence underlines a similar
irresponsibility in De Flores himself; this is not the breakdown
of Beatrice alone, but also, as we shall see later, the beginning of
De Flores' self-destruction.

Beatrice makes a swift recovery. To turn aside unpleasantness
with a joke and a gift graciously bestowed is part of the breeding
of a fine lady; the keeper has his fees at a stag-hunt and the dia-
mond is his to 'make use on'. Whereupon De Flores delivers his
second thrust:

> 'Twill hardly buy a cap-case for one's conscience though,
>   To keep it from the worm, as fine as 'tis.

[III.4.45]

This maidenly image, incongruously associated with conscience and the worm, is a sharp reminder of their joint act, which Beatrice again tries to parry with placatory suggestions. But her confidence is at last undermined when De Flores dismisses her ill-considered little plan for his flight with sound logic:

> You must fly too then . . .
> Come your fears counsel you but ill; my absence
> Would draw suspect upon you instantly.
>
> [III.4.82–7]

Here is the first indication of De Flores' sinister efficiency; he is a born organiser, knowledgeable in everything that concerns the exclusively material side of life—hence his power over those who lack his acumen. Driven from her guard, Beatrice admits that 'he speaks home', and De Flores presses his advantage to scatter the last defences of the fine lady—birth, dignity, and her wonted virtue, the last so long unquestioned in her sheltered life that not even murder, so long as it is at second hand, can shake her conviction that it still exists. Every feminine retort De Fores returns with a new connotation that reverses her position. She rebukes him for forgetfulness, whereupon he reminds her that she herself is forgetful in a deeper sense. She rebuffs his advances with an appeal to modesty which he unmasks for the pretence that it is— 'A woman dipp'd in blood, and talk of modesty!'; and when she reminds him of the distance set between them by 'creation', De Flores aptly plays upon her words, upon the idea of re-creation— on his level, not on hers—on the implications of her own reference to 'such another deed', the deed which she has foolishly hoped to father on him, until he has her where he wishes, in a reciprocity of degradation:

> . . . settle you
> In what the act has made you; you're no more now.
> You must forget your parentage to me . . .
> . . . and I challenge you,
> As peace and innocency has turn'd you out,
> And made you one with me.
>
> [III.4.135–41]

The absolute moral justice that De Flores here projects is the more impressive for the harshness with which it is associated. It is a dominant element in the play; Beatrice will meet it again in the

judgment of Alsemero, 'so clear in understanding', which she
dreads, and De Flores himself will encounter it—and falter—in
his victim's brother and in the ghost which comes between him
and the star.

In this play and to a lesser extent in *Women Beware Women*,
the moral realities fulfil the function of fate in classical tragedy;
it is in this sense that De Flores, who most clearly voices them, is
indeed the meteor on which, Beatrice declares, her destiny has
hung. Yet De Flores is no symbolic figure; his frustrated humanity is implied throughout the scene in a sequence of impressions,
as the dramatic tempo rises (l.98ff.)—I'm in pain and must be
eased of you . . . I was as greedy on't As the parch'd earth of
moisture . . . I have thrown contempt upon your gold, Not that I
need it not . . . my life I rate at nothing'. His physical and emotional neediness, his lust, his elation, his pain, his determination to
have satisfaction at all costs, these human needs which Beatrice in
disgust at his physical exterior has ignored, call her to account as
the scene closes.

Her obsessional hatred of De Flores is the obverse of a fascination which he is quick to exploit. His whole project is based on the
assumption that neither love nor hate has any meaning beyond
the physical, and that once she has come to rely on him for help
revulsion will turn into desire. By the end of the scene he has
sufficiently mastered her protests to prophesy that she will come to
love what she 'faints to venture on'. When we see them together
again her expressions of admiration are only half ironical:

> The east is not more beauteous than his service
>
> [V.1.71]
>
> A wondrous necessary man
>
> [V.1.90]
>
> Here's a man worth loving
>
> [V.1.93]

The sexual affinity, unnameable to Beatrice, underlying the
growing kinship between the two conspirators is dispassionately
assumed in the imagination of De Flores. Again the sinister nature
of their relationship derives from their inability to communicate.

Middleton's presentation is psychologically unerring. In later
scenes the split in Beatrice's affections is paralleled by the contradiction between her moral assumptions and her actual conduct.

She can still cling to maidenly notions of decorum, still rebuke Diaphanta for immodestly enjoying the use she makes of her to cover her own reputation, still prudently demur at endangering property when De Flores proposes setting a room on fire for the same reason. Meantime her compliance becomes absolute and we hear her helpless dependence upon his better judgment in her whimpered reply when he rebukes her for trusting a waiting-woman—'I must trust somebody' (V.1.15). Once more her schemes for safety come to nothing in practice; again she miscalculates the human element, and again it is De Flores who comes to her aid with an expedient which saves the situation only to bind her more closely to him.

The scene in which Beatrice, shivering in her night-gown, waits for Diaphanta to come from her bridegroom that she may take her place, is built upon a crescendo of anxiety.[7] Beatrice is like a taut string and De Flores plays upon her, while the striking clocks, punctuating their whispered conversation, suggest the night stillness as well as the passage of time. At the climax of suspense De Flores exclaims:

> . . . look, you're undone;
> The day-star, by this hand.
>
> [V.1.25]

The day-star, associated with the beauteous east, the impression of cold and trembling, the shadow that passes before the star—all invoke the chill of an early morning, but it is more than a piece of skilful stage direction. Against the pleasant dawn associations the significance of what the first daylight can mean for Beatrice links back to her dread of Alsemero's 'clear understanding'. For Beatrice the nature of light as of other good things begins to be reversed, and in the half ludicrous turn of circumstances she comes to realise the frustration of her marriage, exclaiming as the phantom obscures the star: 'Some ill thing haunts the house' (V.1.62).

It is precisely because the situation borders on the absurd that we can credit Beatrice's acceptance at this point of De Flores' new assertion of power over her mind as well as her body:

> How heartily he serves me! his face loathes one;
> But look upon his care, who would not love him?
>
> [V.1.70]

And a few minutes later when, on being reminded of the embraces which Diaphanta has enjoyed in her stead, she throws off all pretence at mourning her death with—'now you tie me: Were it my sister, now she gets no more'—we hear the Beatrice who will sardonically accept the division in her own nature with the frank admission to Alsemero that his love has made her 'a cruel murderess'. Step by step the logic of circumstances drives her to her own self-dismissal as a corruption in her father's blood to be cast away for his 'better health'.

Middleton was perhaps learning from Rowley, but his theatre sense in this scene is worth noting. The passages quoted have the effect of spotlighting on the modern stage or of the isolation of detail in a film close-up. The day-star dominates the dialogue with the potency of a visible object, like the symbolic properties which Webster uses in *The White Devil*.[8] But Middleton's treatment is of such delicacy and restraint that we are conscious only of the effect and scarcely at all of the means used. Middleton could never incur the charge of sensationalism; he was incapable of employing a concept beyond its usefulness to meaning, and to meaning rather than to the enrichment it might confer in itself.

The restraint with which he can paint a scene is also a distinguishing mark in his handling of character. Nothing could more clearly demonstrate the gulf between Middleton and his contemporaries in tragic drama—or for that matter, more fully illustrate the effect of his early training in satirical comedy—than the treatment of his heroine in *The Changeling*. The obvious parallels are with Vittoria in *The White Devil* and Ford's Annabella in *'Tis Pity She's a Whore*. But Vittoria is conceived on an exalted level, a princess indeed, imprisoned in a situation out of tune with her high spirit, inspiring men to act on her behalf, sinning, loving and being loved, all on a grand scale. Beatrice on the other hand is a managing little person, persisting in taking the initiative with people and with forces beyond her understanding. Vittoria is a magnanimous rebel, Beatrice is merely cocksure.

Ford's Annabella has something of Beatrice's simplicity coupled with innate high principle; like her she is betrayed by passion into an intolerable predicament, but Annabella's suffering so stirs the depths of her nature, so strengthens and defines her personality, as to bring her to a maturity of spirit sufficient to inspire her lover to resolution, and this in the moment when the breakdown of her false assumptions leaves her exposed only to her death. But Beatrice is brought to face in herself something which only her childishness has obscured from her hitherto. Beatrice's story is a slow disenchantment, always coloured with a touch of the ridiculous.

This underlying absurdity, which he had used to such effect in the serious episodes of *A Fair Quarrel*, brings him closer in spirit to Ibsen[9] and the moderns than to his immediate colleagues. In the exhilaration which passes for passion, because it blinds her to consequences against the evidence of her senses, Beatrice comes nearer to Hedda Gabler than to Vittoria or Annabella. Her view of life is as naïve as Hedda's, and this naïvety leads her to believe as Hedda believes when she burns the manuscript, that peace of mind can be secured by the physical removal of that which offends her. But more important in both characters is their fundamental mediocrity contrasted with the height of their aspirations, and particularly in their choice of lover. The glimpse we have of Alonso suggests the unreflective, ordinary man, whereas Alsemero sets a standard which to Beatrice is both disturbing and compelling, and like Hedda she is betrayed by her illusions into a situation which mocks her preconceived notions of the world she thought she knew.

The treatment of Alsemero is unusual in Middleton, though it bears some relation to that of Captain Ager's idealism. Alsemero's function in the play is to project an absolute standard of morals and rationality which grows in impressiveness as the action develops. We see Alsemero not as a character in the round but in a series of sharp, thumbnail sketches. When he falls in love it is 'to the holy purpose'; later he alone has the discernment to see the danger in De Flores' haunting of Beatrice, and as the nuptial night approaches it is not his lover's tenderness but his uncompromising integrity that weighs upon Beatrice so that she falters from one folly to another. Until the last ignominy—that of discovery —falls upon Beatrice, Alsemero is given little to say; then he speaks with the relentlessness of judgment. It is Alsemero who places the other characters where they belong and finally it is he who sums up the meaning of the play. In Alsemero there is no wit, no humour, no equivocation; he speaks as he acts, with a plain truthfulness which, like the evil in De Flores, is a little removed

from the human level, but which the placing of his rare entrances
and the pattern of the play induce us to accept as an aspect of
character.

At the climax of the play Alsemero and De Flores stand in
relation to Beatrice as polar opposites. When Beatrice 'couples',
not with what she admires and values above all else, but with
what she most abhors, while at her own devising a waiting-
woman usurps her marriage joys, her nature is reversed, an irony
that goes deeper even than Hedda's discovery of her own futility.

It is in De Flores that this irony is always half vocal—in his
adherence to fact, the fact of his own physiognomy 'to a hair and
pimple', in face of Beatrice's pretence that he looks 'amorously',
as well as to the fact of their partnership in murder as against her
short-lived triumph. Middleton had many precedents for De
Flores. The late Elizabethan drama is prolific of parasites and
malcontents, standing solitary among the other characters, well
skilled in fending for themselves. The careful association of De
Flores with poison[10] is in the tradition and he touches the stock
character at several points. Yet his discontent springs exclusively
from his own make-up; it owes nothing to his circumstances,
needy as they are, and can be satisfied only through the passions
and the instincts. It is to Middleton's credit that he can present
this avid and tormented figure without a trace of the senti-
mentality which often solicits sympathy for the Malcontent in
Jacobean drama. De Flores regrets his ugliness even less than does
Shakespeare's *Richard III*, and his circumstances not at all; both
are facts to be reckoned with, but with a detachment which is
somehow *less* than human.

His position in Vermandero's household is not unlike that of
Iago in the entourage of Othello; he is full of service, it is his
luck to be 'i'th' way still' and it is on him that Vermandero calls
when anything practical is to be done, from the retrieving of a
dropped glove, to dealing with a fire in the house.

> That fellow's good on all occasions.
>
> [V.1.89]

As Roderigo to Iago, the weaker nature turns to De Flores and
the innocent trust him;[11] he is 'honest De Flores' to Tomaso, his
victim's brother, as Iago is 'honest' to Othello, and his vigorous
enjoyment of illicit action—'How this fire purifies wit!'—is akin

to Iago's satisfaction at the uproar he has engendered in Cyprus:

> Pleasure and action make the hours seem short.
> [*Othello*, II.2]

But in contrast De Flores never dissembles. This is his strength; he is moved only by desire, whereas the motives actuating the traditional Malcontent—ambition, jealousy, self-love—have no place in his nature. He aspires to one thing alone, the physical enjoyment of the object of his obsession. It is this 'travelling light' that places him in the position of observer, yet his vision is focused upon Beatrice. Indeed the Malcontent's general comments would have no relevance in this play, where the scope of the action is designedly limited and where the dramatic function of De Flores is not to relate the situation to a wider significance, but to underline its essential unreality.

Yet if, in the conception of Allwit, Middleton seemed here and there to recall that of Webster's Flamineo, the association is even stronger in the presentation of De Flores. In the latter's searching comments on Beatrice's self-delusion, we have something of the worldly wisdom of Flamineo. De Flores' management of Beatrice's affairs, as efficient as Flamineo's pandarism or Allwit's opportunism, his attitude of contemptuous forbearance to those whose interests he serves for his own ends, may again be suggested by the same source; and his concern for Beatrice's marriage joys, half comic, half satanic, is of the nature of Flamineo's ironic guardianship of his sister's romance. In the growing familiarity of his comments on the wedding night:

> Sure the devil
> Hath sowed his itch within her; who would trust
> A waiting woman?
> [V.1.13]

and the slight leer in his reference to 'our pleasure and continuance', we have again an echo of Flamineo, and there is some parallel with Flamineo's dying admission that his life was 'a black charnel' in De Flores' pun, also at the moment of death, 'I coupled with your mate At barley-break; now we are left in hell' (V.3.165). Flamineo's arrogant determination, Lodovico's defiant

singlemindedness,[12] both typical attitudes in Revenge Tragedy,
are echoed in his claim:

> . . . her honour's prize
> Was my reward; I thank life for nothing
> . But that pleasure.
>
> [V.3.170]

It would be a mistake, however, to attribute to Middleton
direct imitation of Webster, or indeed of any other dramatist. In
turning back to the themes of early Jacobean tragedy in this play
it was natural that he should write in the spirit, though not after
the model, of *The White Devil* which had been published twelve
years previously. If therefore the weakening of De Flores in later
scenes recalls Webster's handling of Flamineo towards the end
of that play, the difference is striking. Twice De Flores is brought
up against his victim's brother and he is nearly self-betrayed at
Alsemero's direct question:

> What's this blood upon your band, De Flores?
> DE FLORES : Blood! no sure 'twas wash'd since.
>
> [V.3.96]

All this is made to stem from the appearance of the ghost which
'takes away the light' and which he dismisses as a 'mist of conscience'. Flamineo is also disturbed by the vision of Brachiano
who appears to him immediately he has witnessed, and been
shaken by, his mother's grief for the brother he has killed. It is
a vulnerable moment, for in encountering the ghost throwing
earth upon him and thereby evoking his question as to how long
he has to live, Flamineo faces not only his conscience but his
mortality. Indirectly the passage is a comment on a way of life.
In contrast Middleton's object is to keep the situation rather
on the comic than the tragic level. For De Flores the encounter
throws up the fundamental weakness, not of humanity, but of
his own character and behaviour, typical and all too human as
these may be. In fact De Flores is initially as self-deluded as his
partner and his fears are as much a part of the theme as is the
latter's frustrated nuptial night. De Flores rushes into murder as
irresponsibly as Beatrice, dazzled with the certainty that the
woman who has loathed him hitherto will now yield herself
entirely because she needs him:

> Methinks I hold her in mine arms already,
> Her wanton fingers combing out this beard,
> And being pleased, praising this bad face.

[II.2.149]

In the word 'pleased' we have Middleton's discernment of possible inherent childishness in the most astute contriver.

Superficially De Flores is proved right, but it is the depth of human nature that always eludes him and that finally betrays him. De Flores argues by fact; he knows nothing of the intuitions that visit Alsemero and Tomaso, or of the growing complexity in Beatrice or of the strength of the retributive justice, the logical outcome of his crime, which the phantom projects. That he 'tumbled into the world a gentleman' is the only parallel we have with Flamineo's handicapped entrance into the world of ambition; beyond that we know only of his office and the use he makes of it. Flamineo's nature is warped by circumstances and Webster makes us feel the pity of it; the breakdown of Flamineo is seen as a process of mortification and primarily a spiritual experience. But De Flores has no pride of flesh to mortify, and therefore the 'mist of conscience' is no more than a temporary setback, the first presentiment that his affairs may not run according to plan.

It is this streak of the commonplace that William Empson seems to ignore in his interesting association of De Flores with the goblin changeling[13] of folk-tale—the subhuman, cunning intruder, who will not act until invited, but will then use his opportunity to 'snatch' his victim to himself. The parallel is illuminating, but De Flores appals, not because of his sinister power over those who turn to him, but because he combines that power with a fallibility which is all too recognisable. Fundamentally, as the development of the action reveals him, De Flores is an ordinary man with the ordinary man's efficiency. What is not ordinary is Middleton's apprehension of the strength of the passions which drive him, and of the extent of suffering of which ordinary men and women are capable, without hope or vision beyond the scope of their limitations. But all this is presented with absolute impartiality, without appeal either to our sympathies or to our blame. The treatment of De Flores is a masterpiece in restraint, but it is in the method of comedy rather than of tragedy as Webster would have understood it.

The difference between Middleton and Webster is a difference in artistic scope. Of the religious beliefs of either we know nothing, though we may surmise something of Webster's. But Webster as an artist could never conceive characters at once so sensitive and so limited in vision. For Webster life itself came between man and reality: thus in his plays, death is presented as a challenge. For Middleton the business of serious drama was to exhibit the human character within the circumstances of daily life. The discovery of reality was also the discovery of the self within its own limits; the death of the character may be the logical outcome but it has no relevance to the meaning of the play.

It is here that Middleton departs from the tragic convention as most of his contemporaries, including Rowley himself, understood it.[14] Admittedly Alsemero's ruthlessness, the screams of the victims behind the locked closet door and Beatrice's violent and protracted death are in the tradition less of the popular than of the private theatre. It is thus that Montsurry deals with his erring wife in Chapman's *Bussy D'Ambois*, and the whole episode with its harsh, forthright justice is in the manner of Marston's tragedies of revenge rather than of those of Webster or Rowley. Yet the similarity is in method alone; tragedy as Marston or Chapman knew it had little lasting influence on his work, but neither, on the other hand, does he follow Webster with whom as a poet-dramatist he has more in common. Middleton's presentation is not the conflict between passion and power but the unmasking of lust by the logic of commonplace happenings. His interest is in retribution rather than revenge, and the retribution he postulates arises from the pressure of consequences and the impact of one personality upon another. Tomaso has no concern with revenge in the conventional sense; he is content if justice is done and shows no desire to be its instrument. Finally it is the two criminals who, significantly, destroy one another.

For characters so conceived the spiritual purgations of tragedy have no place. When after a series of chance incidents—gossip overheard, the discovery from a window of Beatrice in intimate conversation with De Flores—the two offenders have met their punishment, Alsemero comments significantly upon the nature of justice as seen in the play. Turning to the now satisfied Tomaso he remarks: 'Sir you are sensible of what truth hath done.' (V.3.188) It is the pressure of reality, not of destiny, that tries

the human spirit; but in Middleton's scheme of things men and
women are less tempted to sin than beguiled by their fears and
follies. Great sinners are as rare as saints; but the tragic emphasis
is on the fact that it is little men who have to face unaided the
enormous consequences of their unconsidered actions.

From this viewpoint the title of the play is apt. The irony on
which it is built is that not only of evasion, but secondarily of
what Hardy would have called the 'deformed intention'. It is a
mis-reading to associate the word 'changeling' exclusively with
the disguised lovers in the sub-plot; in fact the idea of reversal
is implied in the opening scene in the contrast between Alsemero's
pledging of his love to a 'holy purpose' and the snapping of
Beatrice's control when De Flores comes upon her, as well as in
her regretting her five days old promise to marry Alonso.
Alsemero's comment on the weather-vane which he observes
turning 'full in my face' again suggests it, and in the last scene,
it is Alsemero who develops the same idea of 'change', with
reiterated emphasis on the word, under the influence of the moon:

> What an opacous body had that moon
> That last chang'd on us! Here's beauty chang'd
> To ugly whoredom; here servant obedience
> To a master sin, imperious murder;
> I, a suppos'd husband, chang'd embraces
> With wantonness . . .
> Your change is come too, from an ignorant wrath
> To knowing friendship.
>
> [V.3.199]

So far the change in Tomaso, from wrath to friendship with
those who are hurt as much as himself, is the only change for
the better, but Isabella now applies the same concept to the
future behaviour of her jealous husband Alibius:

> ISABELLA: your change is still behind,
>   But deserve best your transformation . . .
> ALIBIUS: I see all apparent wife, and will change now
>   Into a better husband.
>
> [V.3.212–17]

Meantime, though in a lighter vein, the transformed courtiers
Antonio and Franciscus make a similar admission:

ANTONIO: I was changed too from a little ass as I was to
              a great fool as I am . . .
FRANCISCUS: I was changed from a little wit to be stark mad.
                                          [V.3.207–11]

The motive of reversal, sometimes cathartic, sometimes merely
ironic, is basic to the play, and loosely knit as it is the under-
plot is designed to make its contribution.[15]

That Rowley may have written passages in both the opening
and the closing scenes is the more significant.[16] He certainly had
a share in the sub-plot and it is possible that both authors regarded it as a comment from a different angle upon the events in
the main plot. Like Beatrice Isabella, wife to Alibius who keeps
a school for fools and madmen, is tempted to become a 'whore
in her affection'. She is visited by two admirers, the one disguised
as a fool, the other as a madman, and all three are closely watched
by Lollio, assistant to Alibius,[17] as De Flores watches Beatrice
and Alsemero. Like De Flores taking advantage of the heroine's
probable fall from honour, Lollio is determined to make use of
Isabella if she should yield to either lover: 'you perceive that I
am privy to your skill; if I find you minister once and set up
the trade, I'll put in for my thirds'.[18] There is a certain inverted
parallelism with the plot against Alonso's life in the main
story, when Isabella warns Lollio that unless he remains silent
'his injunction for me enjoying, shall be to cut thy throat'
(III.2.254). We hear much of the moon, but the 'opacous moon'
with its sinister suggestions in Alsemero's speech quoted above
becomes in the sub-plot the fantastic moon of fairy tale—the
'waning moon', the 'big-bellied moon'—and whereas 'some ill
thing haunts the house' of Vermandero (V.1.67), in that of
Alibius 'tis but a fool that haunts the house' (IV.3.207).

Shrewd and calculating as he is, Lollio like De Flores is
described as 'honest' and Isabella's sensible handling of her admirers and of her jealous husband is a foil to the behaviour of
Beatrice. Meantime the metamorphosis of the lovers into idiot
and madman has in its context a certain implied comment on
the more serious folly of Alonso and Alsemero.

These parallels are too numerous and too significant on their
own level to be disregarded, and they are as carefully planned
as the patterning of Middleton's comedies. To play the tragic

story of the main plot against a background of lunacy, with all the possibilities the latter offered for the contemporary theatre in dance, song, dumb show and other popular devices, is dramatically significant and was at the same time well suited to performance at a court where the masque was in fashion.[14] Antonio's role of harmless idiot or 'innocent' might appeal to a circle in which natural fools were still not unknown as household pets, while Isabella's disguise as madwoman could furnish, with Antonio in similar disguise, a *pas de deux* on almost formal ballet lines. The scene (IV.3) in which this last incident occurs ends with a dance of fools and madmen, intended as a rehearsal for the festivities at Beatrice's wedding which we never see. Nevertheless the madmen have already been given sufficient prominence to make their dance effective as an ironic comment on the events of the nuptial night to which it serves as prelude.[20]

Again the dumb show, though above all characteristic of Middleton's determination to telescope anything not strictly relevant to his theme, would have its place in the spectacle demanded of a performance at Court. The masque convention is traceable throughout the play—in the burlesque of the main theme in the sub-plot, even in the hint of comic contrast with which the 'change' assumed by Antonio and Franciscus is referred to in the closing scene. From this angle the 'school' of fools and madmen is the visible ironic counterpart to Beatrice's own background. In fact the construction of the play as a whole, with its careful alternating of episodes from the main and subsidiary plots, its recurring parallelism of group with group and character with character—Beatrice with Isabella, De Flores with Lollio, Alsemero and Jasperino with the opposing pair Alonso and Tomaso, the Governor's castle with the lunatic asylum —all underlines the impression of absurdity in the behaviour and situation of the central figures.[21] The two sides of the play are complementary and mutually explanatory so that, as Mr. Bawcutt comments: 'what is implied in the main plot becomes literal in the sub-plot'.[22] Clearly the sub-plot is an integral part of the author's design, but whatever the correct distribution of the text may be it seems likely that the play's overall conception was the work of one mind.

The integrity of the design as a whole is reflected in much of the imagery. Middleton is generally little given to sensory images,

but the majority of the visual concepts in the play are schematic
in the contrast they suggest between what is normal or accepted
and what is unpleasant or frightening; as in the action, so in the
image horror is enhanced by being presented within the commonplace or in the setting of normal associations. The contrast may
be within the image itself as when, in a passage quoted above,
De Flores warns Beatrice that the ring which she bestows on
him will 'hardly buy a capcase for one's conscience', substituting
in the following line, the word 'worm' for the moth more naturally
associated with the usefulness of a capcase. Or again when he
avers that her

> . . . shooting eye
> Will burn my heart to cinders.
>
> [III.4.152]

where after the conventional image of the 'shooting eye', the
slight shock of 'cinders' has an effect opposite to that expected
and brings us nearer to the idea of hell than to that of the conventional lover's heaven. Or the concept itself may be incongruous
as when De Flores, to whom most of these images are given,
exclaims of Beatrice:

> A woman dipp'd in blood and talk of modesty!
>
> [III.4.127]

or as when Alsemero rebukes her on her confession of the murder:

> O, thou should'st have gone
> A thousand leagues about to have avoided
> This dangerous bridge of blood!
>
> [V.3.80]

In both the effect of suspense is gained, however, not only by
the startling quality of the image itself—'*dipp'd* in blood', '*bridge*
of blood', but also by its association with something either re-
assuring or normal—with 'modesty' in the first instance and in
the second with an everyday course of action, as when a wise
man avoids a danger by taking a journey round 'about'.

This baroque use of the image Middleton may well have
learnt from Webster, but whereas Webster was sometimes betrayed by the fascination which it had for him into the over-
emphasis which many of his critics have unfairly exaggerated,

Middleton has these images so completely under the control of
his dramatic intention, that the words leap into meaning without
passage of developed imagery in which Beatrice admits her guilt
a superfluous syllable. A good example of this control is the
to Vermandero:

> I am that of your blood was taken from you
> For your better health; look no more upon't,
> But cast it to the ground regardlessly,
> Let the common sewer take it from distinction.
>
> [V.3.153]

The idea of blood-letting, so dear to the Jacobeans and to
Webster in particular, is stated succinctly and developed with
ruthless logic, but it is the operant words, not the emotional
associations of the image, that carry the meaning—'regard-
lessly', 'common', 'take it from distinction'—a summary of
Beatrice's whole unlucky history and a fair impression of what
she experiences now of failure and disillusionment; but it is all
on the level of fact. Webster would have touched the 'common
sewer' into a figment of self-loathing; with Middleton it is merely
'common'.

The difference in method may be seen when De Flores exclaims
of the act he has committed in Beatrice's service:

> I was a greedy on't
> As the parch'd earth of moisture when the clouds weep.
>
> [III.4.108]

Webster has a not dissimilar passage which Middleton may have
known.

> Instruction to thee
> Comes like sweet showers to over-harden'd
> ground;
> They wet but pierce not deepe.
>
> [*The White Devil* IV.3.125]

In the quotation from *The White Devil* more is implied than is
stated. The placing of 'sweet showers', with its extraneous associations of spring rain and freshness, in the context of 'over-
harden'd' suggests an offered grace. Brief as the passage is, the
image carries certain religious overtones which grow in the

imagination. Middleton, on the other hand, subordinates the
entire concept to the idea of greed; its effect is in its economy.
The substitution of the more clearly defined impressions of
'moisture' and 'parch'd earth for those of 'sweet showers' and
'over-harden'd ground' divests the image of all but purely
physical associations so as to focus sharply upon the speaker's
insatiable desire. It is this writing under pressure that gives to
the play the incandescent quality which Mr. Schoenbaum notes
when commenting on the verse dialogue of *The Revenger's
Tragedy*.[23]

Nevertheless this austere control has a restrictive effect on
Middleton's vision of humanity in this play. Out of their limited
scope the characters speak with a sharpened urgency, but we
see neither Beatrice nor De Flores whole; both represent facets
of typical people in a particular situation which Middleton's
sustained imagination induces us to accept as from life, and they
are surrounded by figures in even slighter profile. We never come
to know Beatrice as we know Vittoria, or De Flores as we know
Flamineo or Iago, nor is it the dramatist's intention that we
should. Middleton's genius is under voluntary restraint, a discipline which gives his writing its incisive power but withholds
him as yet from the fullest tragic experience.

He is still preoccupied with those facts of life which a moment
of crisis can illumine. What he sees of human fallibility he can
state with clarity and integrity, but investigation of the deeper
complexities of motive and behaviour was to come in *Women
Beware Women*. Middleton can dissect with the delicate touch
of a surgeon's fingers, but his tendency is still to analyse rather
than to create. Yet he had already given a new emphasis to
tragic drama and his refusal to interpose himself between the
play and its meaning to make an acceptable conclusion is part
of that purpose. Alsemero's epilogue is chilling but carefuly
calculated:

> All we can do to comfort one another,
> To stay a brother's sorrow for a brother,
> To dry a child from the kind father's eyes,
> Is to no purpose.
>
> [V.3.224]

and the lines are the more effective in being spoken by the

character in aspiring to whose level Beatrice has destroyed herself. There is no catharsis here, no passion spent; this is the tragedy of reversal and it is human good intention that is reversed.

In thus penetrating the experience of ordinary people in circumstances they can neither understand nor control, Middleton had employed the methods and to some extent the matter of comedy to broaden the scope of tragedy. How much of this development may be attributed to his association with Rowley we shall never know. As an actor-dramatist Rowley was a theatre man in a sense in which Middleton was not, and his instinct for quickening the action with noise and bustle just when the tempo requires it is of some importance in *The Changeling*. The variety of pace and tone in the longer sustained episodes here and in *Women Beware Women* Middleton may well have learned from him. But more important is the new element of compassion, which informs *A Fair Quarrel* and shapes a good deal of *The Changeling*; in both plays there is a sense of released imagination and a widening of vision. Undeniably it was in association with Rowley that Middleton found his proper bent in the popular theatre and it was with Rowley that he began to formulate a new kind of tragedy. In his next play he would carry the experiment a stage further.

5. *Women Beware Women*

Women Beware Women sets a problem for the critic as well as the producer. In the workmanlike handling of a double plot and the sensitive treatment of a wide range of characters the play is a development from *The Changeling*, and the first four Acts are a model of construction and dramatic control. But in the fifth Act, where it should reach its resolution, the action stops short or seeps away into 'staginess'. The ultimate impression is either that Middleton ran out of material or, conversely, that he had more to say but simply could not find the means to say it.

Yet *Women Beware Women* has links with *The Changeling* in its emphasis on those primitive instincts which are basic to Middleton's view of life, and in a recognition of fundamental moral sanctions which we find increasingly in his characteristic work. And again, as in *The Changeling*, Middleton tends to shape his sources to something like the pattern of the popular tale.

The real Bianca Capello had left her mark on the history of the Italian States in the influence which she exercised first as mistress, then as Duchess to Francesco d'Medici, Duke of Florence.[1] Born of a noble Venetian family, Bianca foolishly eloped with Pietro Buonaventura, a Florentine youth of humble extraction and poor circumstances. Catching sight of her on the balcony of her husband's house, Francesco fell in love with her, made her his mistress through the offices of Madrigone, a Florentine nobleman, and apparently persuaded Pietro into acquiescence on the promise of improvement in his social and financial status. Whereupon Pietro began an illicit affair of his own with a rich widow, an association of which he boasted openly and in spite of the remonstrations of Bianca herself, who seems to have been genuinely concerned for his safety. Finally a nephew of the widow, a hot-blooded young man like Middleton's Hippolyto, challenged him to a duel in which Pietro was killed, leaving the way open for Bianca's marriage with Francesco.

But the Duke's younger brother, Cardinal Ferdinando d'Medici, remained hostile to the marriage, and on his refusal to recognise the legitimacy of her son by the Duke, Bianca prepared a poisoned marchpane (according to Fynes Moryson) of which the Duke himself inadvertently partook. Thus betrayed, Bianca eagerly ate of the same dish, leaving Ferdinando to inherit the Dukedom.

It is with evident purpose that Middleton makes of Leantio, the Pietro of the original story, not another Allwit, but a simple unschooled young man, betrayed by his own limitations as well as by those of circumstances—entrusting his bride in the first flush of married happiness to the care of his mother, oblivious in his own obtuseness to the effect that a changed environment may have in his absence. Leantio is too piteous to blame. Pietro's affair with the rich widow has its counterpart in Leantio's dazed acceptance, on Bianca's defection, of the advances of Livia, sister to Hippolyto, but when Leantio bursts into Bianca's apartments in the Ducal Palace, his bragging about his new-found affluence is not the expression of Renaissance Italian arrogance, but the overflowing of a weak nature hurt in its tenderest part.

Now this suggests an outlook on human character broader than in the comedies and yet more penetrating than in *The Changeling*. After the shrewd study of the willing cuckold in *A Chaste Maid in Cheapside* Pietro's story could have formed the basis of a dramatic conflict between love and necessity; instead Middleton concentrates attention on Leantio's helplessness, which both makes Bianca's degradation certain and fires desire in Livia. On the other hand, the emphasis on the commonplace domestic background, the entrusting of the stolen bride to the foolish old mother, the uncouth silliness of the bridegroom, so far removed from his bride in birth and breeding, Bianca's complaints of the restrictions put upon her by Leantio's jealous anxiety—all this has a cautionary significance which could find a place in folktale. Leantio's misplaced confidence is in the same tradition.

> . . . what assurance
> Of this restraint then? Yes, yes, there's one with her:
> Old mothers know the world, and such as these
> When sons lock chests are good to look to keys.
>
> [I.1.173]

The story of Isabella and Hippolyto in the secondary plot is from a French novel not translated until 1627.[2] As in the novel

Hippolyto falls in love with his niece Isabella, who at first repels his advances but is tricked by Hippolyto's widowed sister into the belief that he is of no kin to her. Using as a blind her marriage, at the insistence of her avaricious father Fabricio, to a rich but foolish young ward, Isabella pursues an incestuous relationship with Hippolyto until circumstances combine to reveal the truth of her situation.

In general outline Middleton followed his sources, but it was with a touch of genius that he linked the two stories in Livia, his version of the widow with whom Pietro found consolation. In the play she is sister to Fabricio and Hippolyto and we see her first in Fabricio's home, but it is in her own house that Guardiano, identified with Madrigone the Duke's follower of the original story, lodges with the Ward, Isabella's foolish suitor, and it is here that the same character with her connivance arranges the meeting between the Duke and Bianca. It is Livia also who, in sympathy with her favourite brother Hippolyto, betrays Isabella into incest, so that the intrigue of the double plot is the product of the same fertile brain. The immediate effect is of course a sense of unity, but Livia's constant impact upon the action underlines a good deal of the play's intention. Again the balancing in alternate scenes in the first Act, of Bianca's imprudent match with the obvious mis-marriage of Isabella with the Ward, followed by her incestuous liaison with Hippolyto, focuses attention on marriage, its dangers and abuses, at the opening of the play. By the end of the first Act all the characters are established in outline and the action is ready to sweep to its first climax in the banquet scene in Livia's house where Bianca is installed as the Duke's mistress, Isabella's betrothal to the Ward announced and Leantio's love affair with Livia begun.

But it is the end of either heroine that seems to have impressed him most; in both stories Middleton discovers the principle that wickedness preys on itself. The original Bianca willingly eats of her own poisoned marchpane on the discovery that it is the Duke her lover, not the Cardinal her enemy, that her plot has destroyed. With Middleton the marchpane becomes more significantly a cup of poison which stains the mouth so that Bianca can confess: 'A blemished face best fits a leprous soul' (V.2.203). Again the lines spoken by Middleton's Isabella when Livia, in anguish for Leantio's death, reveals the true nature of her relationship with Hippolyto, recalls the despair of the Isabella of the novel eagerly accepting the death by poison to which she is condemned:

> O shame and horror,
> In that small distance from yon man to me
> Lies sin enough to make a whole world perish.
>
> [IV.2.134]

Once more in the double theme, Middleton seizes upon that ironic juxtaposition of dream and reality and the moral ambivalence of human behaviour which he had exposed in *The Changeling*.

This irony gives the play at first sight the slant of classical tragedy. Here, in contrast to *The Changeling* the guilty seem fully conscious of approaching retribution, of the insecurity of their condition even while they sin. In the early scenes Leantio is even in his own eyes not a good son, nor a particularly conscientious factor, nor an entirely worthy husband. First and last he is a thief; 'I see then 'tis my theft; we're both betray'd' (III.1.300), he exclaims when the Duke summons him to the banquet and later, when he witnesses Bianca's perfidy:

> O equal justice, thou hast met my sin
> With a full weight! I'm rightly now opprest,
> All her friends' heavy hearts lie in my breast.
>
> [III.2.94]

Similarly Hippolyto is alive to the degree of his guilt even in his determination to enjoy its fruits. His niece's marriage must go forward as coverage for his own relations with her.

> It is the only veil wit can devise
> To keep our acts hid from sin-piercing eyes.
>
> [II.1.237]

But the expression 'sin-piercing' carries an emphasis that colours his subsequent behaviour.

Yet while this sense of guilt disturbs the dream it does not dissolve it, indeed after every admission the characters retreat still further into their illusory security. So the pricks of conscience are no more than irritants in a process of undoing and degrading.

Leantio's romance fades, Bianca's idealised passion, which made
her bridegroom's poor home a second birthplace, turns into a
kind of lust to be replaced later by another kind of lust, and in
the following action Leantio's hurt affection is soothed by Livia's
lascivious advances and the allure of her weath—all at the mere
touch of adverse circumstances, like the breaking of a spell. In
their new triumph Leantio and Bianca are exposed to one
another's scorn and when the whole truth of Isabella's friendship
with her much-loved uncle is out, Guardiano reduces the issue
to sour comedy with his fear that 'All the world will grin at me'
followed by the Ward's ludicrous outcry: 'O Sordido, Sordido,
I am damn'd, I am damn'd, One of the wicked' (IV.2.79–80).

Middleton's intention is evidently the exposure of a general
lowering of the moral temperature. When the sensitive Hippolyto
apprehends the incestuous nature of his desires he exclaims:

> . . . 'tis most meet that I should rather perish
> Than the decree divine receive least blemish.
> Feed inward, you my sorrows, make no noise,
> Consume me silent, let me be stark dead.
>
> [I.2.157]

Nevertheless now that Heaven has seen how good his intentions
are, he is quite prepared to take advantage of any opportunity
Heaven cares to send in order to indulge his will—

> . . . you see my honesty,
> If you befriend me, so.
>
> [I.2.161]

For the Duke marriage and a contrived murder are easy ways to
salve his conscience and make Bianca honest, and when the latter
assures him, at her husband's expense: 'I love peace, Sir',
Middleton reverses her meaning in the Duke's unconsciously
ironic reply, 'And so do all that love' (IV.1.127).

We hear a good deal about peace. It is the same peace that
Hippolyto acknowledges in his relationship with Isabella as he
leads her out to dance at the banquet: 'Come my life's peace';
the same also that Bianca believed she had found in her first
marriage, 'a quiet peace with this man's love' (I.1.127). It is a
neat expression of that self-evasion combined with a genuine, if

facile, desire for the good life, which was for Middleton a basic
tragic theme, first found in comedy.

Yet all these characters are well-meaning people at the beginning of the play. Isabella, like Bianca, meant 'to keep her
days true to her husband'[3] and Leantio's marriage was to be a
new 'sampler'. Even Livia is impelled to a considerable extent,
whatever her basic motive may be, by kindly impulse and hos-
pitality. But in the event Livia's worldly wisdom is a burlesque
of the precept of moderation. Experience has taught her no more
of womanly dignity than 'discretion'—which should do well
enough for 'a brittle people'. The word 'enough' is recurrent,
but especially in dialogue concerned with Livia. Her bounty 'is
the credit and the glory Of those that have enough' (III.2.245).
'I've enough, Sir' is her assurance to Leantio as she woos him;
what she gives and asks is the average, no more: 'Do you but
love enough, I'll give enough'. Leantio answers with a cynicism
growing upon his conscience, 'Troth then I'll love enough and
take enough', and Livia, 'Then we are both pleased enough'
(III.2.375–7). Curiously the idea is echoed almost exactly, in
Ibsen's trolls in *Peer Gynt* whose watchword is 'enough'.

The situation is a familiar one in many domestic comedies,
but the seriousness of the play's intention is driven home with
unusual deliberation by the appearance of the Cardinal to represent the challenge of conscience, in an incident which recalls
the reversals of the closing scene in *The Changeling*. After the
Duke's ingenious plan to dispose of Leantio at second hand and
so make all safe—'the great cure's past'—the effect of his encounter with his brother is to turn his position inside out. Hitherto
he has disposed of lesser men; now his very greatness, according
to the Cardinal's magnificent analogy of the 'flame upon a
mountain', exposes him by virtue of his responsibility to a greater
spiritual insecurity than theirs. The thin shelter of the flesh,
'but poor thin clay', posed against the terror of eternal torment,
the uncertainty of fortune, the certainty of death, make an apt
reply to the Duke's escapist morality, and the latter's sudden dread
of 'a dearth in grace' underlines the impression of immutable
justice. The Cardinal's revelation is of a state of spiritual naked-
ness; the irony of the situation is that the great man who believed
his will was absolute shrinks from 'a minute's reprehension' and
now takes further refuge in sophistry. Marriage, however

contrived, secures all, and seen through the Cardinal's eyes the pageantry of Bianca's wedding becomes yet another attempt to escape from Heaven's anger in 'worship done to devils'.

Now this general lowering of standards has its counterpart in the scrupulously realistic background to the ill-adjusted lovers in the main story. Whatever the social level mediocrity is its quality, and it is in his social, as well as in his personal mediocrity that Leantio provides a new focus for tragedy. For commonplace as he is, it is in Leantio that the deepest suffering is felt; in contrast to Bianca his every line during their encounter in the palace is tinged with pain and, in addition, a good proportion of the figurative passages are put into his mouth. His relations with his mother are credibly conceived; the widow is made to represent at every appearance the limitations of Leantio's environment, and her moral obtuseness has some kinship with his own restricted vision of life. She is 'full of wants' but necessity has made her content with her lot, and her obsequious simplicity makes her fair game for that social class which is a little above her in breeding.

Then there are the natural simpletons of the middle class, clumsily meddling in delicate matters, true figures of comedy in their ludicrous single-mindedness—the pantaloon Fabricio, testily oblivious of everything save his obstinate determination to marry his daughter to money, the grossly rich young Ward, also oblivious to everything but 'cat and trap' and lechery. And on the cultural upper fringe of their social milieu are their leisured and educated connections, Hippolyto with his illogical moral sense coupled with conventional notions of family honour, Guardiano with his courtier's acumen, Livia with the adroitness of the experienced woman of station. Beyond them, touching their affairs at every point of crisis, is the Court with the Duke at its centre. Here is a widening of scope anticipating *A Game at Chess*. Within the limits of a single play Middleton presents a transection of human character and society with the faithfulness of a camera at close range, yet no character is either entirely ridiculed or entirely condemned; all are presented with an impartiality which tells us nothing of the dramatist's own predilections.

The title covers only half the theme, for the play exposes the hapless state of womanhood as well as women's exploitation of one another. Isabella's story underlines Bianca's experience so

that what appears in the main plot dressed in the semi-domestic
romance of folk-tale is overtly stated in the sub-plot. As distinct
from the sub-plot of *The Changeling* this is an analysis of the
main theme rather than a comment upon it. Middleton's re-
handling in the Ward of the character of the boorish fool, like
Chough to whom Jane Russell was to be married off in *A Fair
Quarrel*, is masterly. Whereas Chough was a good hearted fellow,
harmless in his enthusiasm for wrestling and roaring, the Ward is
an embodiment of the lower man. Almost every line he speaks is
charged with crude sexual significance and, as Roma Gill notes,[4]
his favourite game of 'cat and trap', with the aid of Sordido's
leering comments, has the same suggestion. His complaint at the
banquet that his intended bride might send him 'a gilded bull
from her own trencher, a ram or goat, or somewhat to be nib-
bling' makes a neat climax. To receive titbits from Isabella's
matrimonial trencher is to be his lot—the sexual associations are
obvious. What marriage with such a man would be like we can
surmise from his appraisal of the 'points' of his bride in a scene
of wry, but nonetheless rich comedy (III.3). Now Middleton is at
some pains to suggest much the same attitude to women and
marriage in a bridegroom as dissimilar to the Ward as Leantio.
Like the Ward he has 'such luck to flesh': 'I never bought a
horse but he bore double' (I.3.51–2); and his view of marriage is
clear enough from his childish gloating over the 'unvalued'st
purchase' he has acquired in Bianca and his determination to
keep her both safe and 'in a good way to obedience'. There is
more than a streak of the wife-beater in Leantio!

   Again, after the widow's shrewd misgivings in the opening
scene the presentation of Isabella's lot draws attention to possible
hazards in any marriage choice, and the danger to which she is
exposed in Hippolyto's incestuous love is a dark counter-sugges-
tion to the easy domesticity of Bianca's homecoming. Isabella's
comment that

> When women have their choices, commonly
> They do but buy their thraldoms, and bring great portions
> To men to keep 'em in subjection; . . .
> Men buy their slaves but women buy their masters.
>
> [I.2.172–9]

and Livia's comparison of the wife to the cook who carries the
dish to her master:

> ... obedience, forsooth, subjection, duty and such kickshaws,
>   All of our making but served in to them
>
> [I.2.42]

are placed so as to sound the keynote of what is to follow. Livia is
always cynically aware of the distinction between the husband's
and the wife's advantage in marriage, and the careless exploitation of women is the theme behind her jocular verbal play on the
chessmen: 'Ho, but they set us on, let us come off As well as we
can poor souls; men care no further' (II.2.271). It is Bianca
however who goes to the heart of the matter when, commenting
upon her fortunes, she criticises the strict upbringing of women:

> ... 'tis not good in sadness
> To keep a maid so strict in her young days.
> Restraint
> Breeds wandering thoughts, as many fasting days
> A great desire to see flesh stirring again:
> I'll ne'er use any girl of mine so strictly.
>
> [IV.1.30]

Bianca's helplessness, which surrenders her to vice, is another
reflection on the position of young women; it is a situation which,
within the social code, naturally betrays one woman to another
as well as to men. Bianca's hardening after her seduction, marked
by an immediate coarsening of speech as she accuses Livia—
'You're a damn'd bawd'—startling as it may be, is the expression
of her plight, which in turn leads her to the cynical conclusion
that she may as well consider herself lost: 'Come poison all at
once' (II.2.431). The brassy exterior of the social lady, when she
first appears as the Duke's mistress at Livia's banquet, though
seemingly far removed from the simplicity of the girl in the opening scene, has been prepared for by her tetchiness with her
mother-in-law and by her assumption of worldly sophistication
at Leantio's return. Similarly her revulsion from the husband she
has betrayed and her near connivance at his death, are the
natural reactions in contemporary Italian society of a violated
personality driven against itself. The gradual deterioration of
character in *The Changeling* under the pressure of circumstances
only partially self-induced, is here reviewed almost exclusively
from the feminine standpoint.

    This is a theme which might easily develop into polemic, but

Middleton handles it as an expression of character, and of character conceived in the round much as it is conceived in *A Fair
Quarrel*. In *The Changeling* character is revealed in flashes of
intense concentration as from a spotlight, and there are similar
instances here—Bianca childishly absorbed on her balcony as the
Duke passes, Fabricio sweating in the cares of fatherhood, the
bored young wife squabbling with her mother-in-law. But here
for the first time in Middleton's work tragic issues are made to
stem directly from the complexities of character on an ordinary
level in the context of normal everyday life.

In Leantio the impoverished but reckess young gallant of
Italian vendetta develops into a sensitive, reflective, but nevertheless limited young factor whose aspirations are beyond either his
means or his natural gifts. Leantio talks the poetry of the commonplace; his mind dwells on analogies, but always from
ordinary experience—the sampler, the store chest to which his
mother keeps the keys, the niggardly work-master who 'never
pays till Saturday night', the dishonest neighbour who will steal
the treasure if he knows of it. His view of Bianca as a commodity,
the rich jewel to be 'cased up from all men's eyes . . . under the
plain roof' (I.1.170 ff.) is the imagining of the typical small
business employee, but it is also poetry. Even so his reflections on
mortality have the touch of his breeding: not the shroud 'stuck
o'er with yew' or even dignified with the current idea of corruption, but 'the toil and griefs of fourscore years Put up in a white
sheet tied with two knots' (I.1.20). His liaison with Livia takes
the form of a bargain and his view of what a good wife should be
is based upon thrift. It is not surprising that this uncertainly
balanced character should waver between common sense—*not*
duty or integrity—and the urge to pleasure, as he leaves the house
after his bride's homecoming. Yet Leantio is aware of and responsive to things beyond his mother's vision; if we see a potential Alibius in the Leantio of the first Act, we also see something of
the sensitivity which will later set up a tension between his new
comforts in Livia and the broken affection which impels him to
seek out his false wife on any pretext. Leantio's simplicity is his
undoing.

In a similarly complex fashion Livia is touched to life. In com-
paring Livia with the 'jolly wife of Bath' Lamb simplifies the
conception out of all recognition. Certainly she is loquacious,

merry at times and often overflowing with the sentimental warmth of the typical large hearted matron. Livia will never be at a loss 'To laugh down time and meet age merrily' (II.2.158). She is a born gossip and busybody, and were she as free of ties as the widow would be 'ever at one neighbour's house Or other all day long' (II.2.187). All men are her spoilt children; women on the other hand are the raw material of her trade. Livia is the typical survivor, widow of two husbands and with a fund of vitality for new alliances. But she is also the typical contriver; a problem quickens her fertile imagination and it is this, rather than compassion—though she is concerned for her brother as she is, in part, for the Duke—that motivates her ensnarement of the younger women. Her virtue is as easy as her affections; her momentary wavering before procuring Isabella for her favourite brother might be a transcript from life:

> Beshrew you, would I lov'd you not so well!
> I'll go to bed and leave this deed undone:
> I am the fondest where I most affect;
>
> [II.1.63]

and she continues dryly,

> This 'tis to grow too liberal.
>
> [II.1.90]

What Lamb has overlooked is her kinship with De Flores. Livia's desires are as savage as they are tainted. There is more than a hint of incest in her petting of Hippolyto, and her wooing of Leantio has a primitive ferocity which we meet again in her denunciation of Isabella as she draws the terrified girl towards her over Leantio's body: 'Look upon me wench . . .' Like De Flores she can play upon human feelings with unerring skill, yet without the slightest understanding of the capacity of the human spirit she trifles with. There can be few examples in English drama of a personality in which pleasure of life, warm-heartedness and wit are so cunningly combined with cruelty and lust to build up a character whose keynote is sheer ignorance of anything beyond her own range of experience. In Middleton's tragedy there is nothing more dangerous than this immaturity of spirit. Like most of his major characters Livia is a child playing with high explosives: to be always meddling is the temptation that pursues and ultimately destroys her, and destroys with her all that she has touched.

There is something of Livia's dubious geniality in the widow, whose affectionate pliability also recalls the Nurse in *Romeo and Juliet*. She is a good thrifty housewife, anxious to do her duty by her son's bride, pleased with a spectacle, responsive to an hour's sociability, though she is a little in awe of the wealthy lady to whom she is 'Sunday dinner woman' and 'Thursday supper woman'. She has the balance and good sense of a kindly neighbour until the prospect of a party overwhelms both her judgment and her moral sense; as Bianca remarks, she would 'trot into a bawd now For some dry sucket or a colt in marchpane' (III.1.269).

Middleton's skill lies partly in knowing when to forget about her—as Shakespeare knew when to forget the Nurse. Professor Oliphant regrets the dropping of this character when Leantio and Bianca are out of her hands,[5] but surely this is another instance of that faithfulness to life which was typical of him at his best. After the climax of Livia's banquet we know and think as little of the widow as Leantio does himself, for we see the subsequent action through his eyes. To reintroduce her, or to bring her to a bad end—as in the unsavoury dismissal of Annabella's unfortunate old nurse in *'Tis Pity She's a Whore*—would be an irrelevance. Had Middleton treated the fortunes of some of the other characters with the same reticence this, in some respects his greatest work, would not have been so marred in its ending.

As in *A Trick* and *A Chaste Maid* this vivid delineation of character is set against an equally vivid background of domesticity, built up both by Middleton's clearly defined conception of his story and by that careful use of the amenities of his stage which we have already seen in *The Widow*. How well we come to know the two dwellings in which, for the most part, Middleton disposes his characters, with an economy approaching that of modern staging: Leantio's house with its inward looking windows where the widow might have sat 'like a drone below' and missed all the fun in the street, the little room concealed off the dark parlour, the upper storey rooms which disappoint Bianca in their lack of garnishings—no cushion cloth of cut work or silken coverlets for the beds; and the balcony giving on to the street— the stage balcony—from which Bianca first sees the Duke. And

Livia's house, where the stage balcony becomes the gallery giving
access to Livia's art treasures and the much talked of 'monument', with the hall and closet, the latter perhaps the inner stage
below, where Livia and the widow play at chess, and where later
Hippolyto challenges Leantio to a duel. Even Bianca's longing for
a bay-window overlooking the 'high street' has some relevance
to the small window stages of the Elizabethan theatre. Middleton's
detailed planning of his background is worthy of Ibsen, as is also
his clear and constant awareness of what he could reasonably
expect of his stage.

It is the same grip upon realistic detail that, to a greater extent
here than in any other play except *A Game at Chess*, stamps the
dialogue with the impress of the speaker. Every major character
speaks with a distinctive voice and with analogies peculiarly his
own. There could hardly be a better impression of a wilful young
woman, rapidly losing her temper with an elder, than the
following:

BIANCA: Never a green silk quilt is there i'th' house, mother
          To cast upon my bed?
MOTHER: No, by troth, is there,
          Nor orange tawny neither.
BIANCA: Here's a house
          For a young gentlewoman to be got with child in!
MOTHER: Yes, simple though you make it, there has been three
          Got in a year in it, since you move me to't,
          And all as sweet faced children and as lovely
          As you'll be mother of . . .
BIANCA: Must I live in want
          Because my fortune match'd me with your son? . . .
                                     I ask less now
          Than what I had at home when I was a maid,
          And at my fathers' house; kept short of that
          Which a wife knows she must have, nay and will—
          Will mother, if she be not a fool born . . .
          You hear me mother.
MOTHER: Ay, too plain, methinks.

                                              [III.1.27]

We catch the rising timbre of the voice, the stamp of the foot, and
the low-toned resentment of the older woman.

Even as unimportant a character as Fabricio speaks with his

own accents in the following passage, where he gives rein to his
excitement at the arrangements for the marriage contract—

FABRICIO: I warrant you for handsome; I will see
               Her things laid ready, every one in order,
               And have some part of her trick'd up tonight.
GUARDIANO: Why well said.
FABRICIO: 'Twas a use her mother had;
               When she was invited to an early wedding,
               She'd dress her head o'ernight, sponge up herself,
               And give her neck three lathers . . .
               On with her chain of pearl, her ruby bracelets,
               Lay ready all her tricks and jiggembobs.
GUARDIANO: So must your daughter.
FABRICIO: I'll about it straight, sir.

                                                       [II.2.64]

Fabricio's pleasure is offset by his obliviousness to the touch of
patronage and barely concealed impatience in Guardiano's brief
replies.

There is a similar sensitivity in the use of imagery. Here more
than in any play before *A Game at Chess* Middleton gives the
image a functional importance, either in building up character or
in defining the significance of the action. The concepts are often
strongly visual, a type of imagery we shall meet again in his next
play, and often so developed as to imply a unifying line of
thought. The extended image given to Hippolyto as he meditates
the removal of Leantio may owe something to Webster, whose
two great tragedies abound in similar passages. Hippolyto sees
himself, not as a virtual assassin, which is what he is, but as a pitiful surgeon putting the patient asleep before amputating a 'lost
limb'. Leantio is the limb, Livia is the patient, and when she
'wakes to honour'

            . . . out of love to her I pity most
            She shall not feel his going till he's lost; . . .
            Then she'll commend the cure.

                                                       [IV.1.175]

How well this passage, offset by the Duke's pun on the word
'cure' which follows—'The great cure's past'—establishes Hippolyto's ponderous reflectiveness, which blinds him to the real
situation. We meet this type of image again in *A Game at Chess*

but it is noticeable that in this play most of these extended images
are given to the three reflective characters, the Cardinal, Leantio
and Hippolyto, and to the last two only when they are deluding
or excusing themselves. The effect is not only to illumine the
speaker's frame of mind but also to economise in dramatic
material. Hippolyto's analogy of the pitiful surgeon telescopes a
debate with himself which could have occupied a considerable
time on the stage.

Similarly Leantio's excitement as he returns, his mind in a
dream world, to his bride of a fortnight, is implied in the wealth
of visual imagery put into his mouth. Expectation becomes the
scent of flowers and instantly his imagination projects the ideal
state of marriage, in a passage which contains a whole sermon in
a single concept.

> . . . a banqueting house set in a garden
> On which the spring's chaste flowers take delight
> To cast their modest odours.
>
> [III.1.90]

Then comes the contrast, so near the nature of his bride if he did
but know it, imaged in the 'fair house built by a ditch-side' and
again, forecasting the 'glorious dangerous strumpet' Bianca is to
become, in the

> . . . goodly temple
> That's built on vaults where carcases lie rotting.
>
> [III.1.98]

Leantio's unsophisticated approach to life, his apprehension of
true worth and the extent of his aspirations, the degree of suffering to which disappointment can drive him, are all suggested,
while the lyricism of first love is to him a 'delicious breath . . . The
violet-bed's not sweeter' and the expected kiss 'As sweet as morning dew upon a rose' (ll. 88, 105). Meantime, as a counter-
suggestion, the city man's appreciation of the inconveniences
awaiting the unwary purchaser of property near the town ditch
familiarises the conception to the speaker's homely level.

This three-fold image briefly defines also the stages of Bianca's
degradation as well as of his own. Already we know that the
lovers have passed from Leantio's banqueting house in the garden, with its suggestion of dignity combined with wholesome

pleasure, to the house by the town ditch—the last a notorious
source of infection; soon, with the Duke, Bianca will take refuge
in the defiled temple which is also the Cardinal's vision of her
marriage. Whether the audience is expected to catch these
references or not, the temple image is emphatic on the stage and
evidently carries a key significance.

The food images used by Isabella in the scene in which Livia
tempts her to incest have a similar functional and economical
effect. In the scene of her first appearance in Fabricio's house
(I.2) Livia follows up her comparison of the wife to a cook serving dishes to her husband by an appraisal of Hippolyto in like
terms— 'thou art all a feast And she that has thee a most happy
guest' (I.2.151–2). Now she sums up her opening hints with an
invitation in the same vein: 'You see your cheer, I'll make you no
set dinner' (II.1.123). The idea of a feast where she may 'taste'
her happiness (II.1.121) is now in Isabella's mind, and the extent
of Livia's domination of her will is demonstrated, without the
necessity of overt statement, in her use of the same image when
she placates Hippolyto on his return:

> When we invite our best friends to a feast
> 'Tis not all sweetmeats that we set before them;
> There's somewhat sharp and salt, both to whet appetite
> And make 'em taste their wine well.
>
> [II.1.198]

Isabella has now become the temptress, and it is again with
Livia's food imagery that she lays before Hippolyto the idea of
their future association:

> She that comes once to be a housekeeper
> Must not look every day to fare well, sir, ...
> She's glad of some choice cates then once a week
> Or twice at most, and glad if she can get 'em.
>
> [II.1.217–224]

At each recurrence the image returns with a new implication, but
the basic association of love with appetite persists. This carefully
extended imagery implies what pages of dialogue could hardly
explain; Livia has done more than tempt, she has transformed
Isabella into a miniature of herself.

Middleton's sense of character and his skill in building up a

situation by suggestion and emotional tension are used to effect
throughout this episode.[6] The personality of the speakers, Livia's
ruthlessness in contrast with Isabella's bewildered innocence,
determines the method of the deception. Livia begins with
motherly sympathy followed by a hint of mystery—'It lies here in
this breast would cross this match' (II.1.92)—and having titil-
lated the girl's natural curiosity she continues to feel round her
predicament with skilful probings until her listener becomes one
tingling nerve of expectation. The incitements of justifiable rebellion, of flattered vanity through her supposed noble parentage, of
freedom to follow inclination, are presented to her in turn. The
assertion that she cannot be 'enforc'd' and the revelation after the
reference to the Marquis of Coria—'You heard the praises of
your father then'—prepare for the undermining of Fabricio's
authority:

> How weak his commands now whom you call father,
> How vain all his enforcements, your obedience.
>
> [II.1.158]

Now that the wonted bonds are loosed Livia can make her final
thrust:

> . . . what a largeness in your will and liberty,
> To take or to reject—
>
> [II.1.160]

followed by the tenuous half query which derives her intention
home: 'or to do both'. It is with calculated irony that Livia now
proceeds to counsel prudence—'All this you've time to think on'
(l.164)—but the less pleasant implications in the following lines
on discretion are softened by the verbal skill which transmutes
them into music.

> O my wench,
> Nothing o'erthrows our sex but indiscretion,
> We might do well else, of a brittle people
> As any under the great canopy.

Middleton's psychological insight is acute. Isabella's mind is
aready fouled by Hippolyto's revelation of his incestuous passion;
the second shock of relief at her supposed remove from him in
blood is well timed to rouse her emotions to the pitch of desire.

Thenceforward, committed as she now is to keeping a secret, Isabella is one of those, who living like Livia by discretion, are also content with 'enough'.

> ... so discretion love me,
> Desert and judgment, I've content sufficient,
>
> [II.1.215]

The nature of Livia's role is aptly stressed by the pun on the word 'aunt', the Elizabethan slang word for bawd—'forget not to call me aunt still'—and in her fiercely reiterated warning to tell none of this to Hippolyto—'Take heed of that ... Do not do't'—we hear the tone of the destroyer who will denounce her victim later.

The word 'bawd' is directly applied to Livia in the next scene, a parallel episode of seduction and perhaps one of the best known in drama of this period. Having wheedled from the widow the secret of her son's marriage, Livia persuades her to send for Bianca whom Guardiano, on the pretext of showing her the house, later betrays to the Duke concealed in the 'monument' in the gallery above. Meanwhile Livia engages the widow in a game of chess.

The verbal play on the chess game in Middleton's probable source for this incident[7] may have suggested his own much closer parallelism between the game of chess and the more serious game being played out above. With Middleton the two games are played out together from start to finish. The 'rook' or 'Duke' appears early in the conversation when the widow complains significantly that 'a paltry rook' comes in her way as Guardiano talks with Bianca. As they go towards the gallery Livia remarks:

> She that can place her man well . . .
> As I shall wench, can never lose her game.
>
> [II.2.299–303]

A few seconds will discover the Duke 'placed' in wait for Bianca. Livia's comments on the chessmen are in fact comments on her own plan of seduction: 'Nay, nay, the black king's mine', and another significant verbal play on the slang variant queen/quean, 'this my queen'. In Livia's duke that 'Will strike a sure stroke for the game anon; Your pawn cannot come back to relieve itself' (II.1.306–7), is foreshadowed the plight of both victims of her cunning, while her jesting at the widow's 'saintish' White King,

'simplicity itself' implies a chilling comment on her real relations
with the characters who cross her path.[8]

At this point Bianca appears above to encounter the Duke, and
the seduction is marked by Livia's cry of triumph, again at the
chess board, 'Did I not say my Duke would fetch you o'er
widow?' (II.1.393). The double situation is still more sharply
defined in the widow's remark: 'You see madam, My eyes begin
to fail' (II.1.397) to which Livia replies: 'I'll swear they do wench
. . . you may see widow How all things draw to an end.'

The episode engages all Middleton's powers of dramatic concentration so that, while game and reality march together point
by point, the whole incident is played out in an easy colloquial
manner. It is a busy varied and natural scene, yet it concentrates
powerfully on Livia, Livia's will and wit and her absolute potency
over those who come within her orbit. And with every line Livia
seems to listen while she plays, alert beneath her sharp comments,
her nerves steady, while the widow hesitates, a prey to uneasiness
which she is too blind and too complacent to define. The action of
the play seems to work up to and stem from this episode, in which
innocence and simplicity are outwitted and the game of chess
seems to typify all the intrigues undertaken by the major characters for inept or illicit purposes. Meantime the two figures sitting
over the chess board while the action revolves round them unite
the dual plot in a common theme.

T. S. Eliot, who thought Middleton had no 'message', evidently felt this episode worth referring to as a comment on the
situation of his own lovers in *The Waste Land*.

> And we shall play a game of chess,
> Pressing lidless eyes and waiting for a knock upon the door.
> [*The Waste Land*. II.137]

The challenge of consequences to human self-evasion grows as the
action progresses until the climax of Livia's denunciation at
Leantio's death. It is in Livia that the play's immediate intention
is most vocal; when over Leantio's body she unmasks Hippolyto
and Isabella she also admits her own guilt:

> It lights upon me now,
> His arm has paid me back upon thy breast.
> [IV.2.75]

Again it is Livia who, like De Flores, is impelled by her own pain to disabuse her fellow sinners. Hippolyto's refusal to face moral issues, his arrogant shift to preserve his honour while carrying on an alliance with his niece, receives a sharper answer than any the Cardinal can give. It is the abyss itself that opens at Livia's reaction to Hippolyto's attempt, carefully rehearsed in the previous scene, to show the 'reason' for his action—'The reason! That's a jest hell falls a-laughing at!' (IV.2.64)—an apt rejoinder to the endemic irresponsibility of all her hearers. After the idealism, the mixed motives, the pleasure, it is in Livia's terms that the characters face reality. Essentially this penultimate climax is complete in itself; what follows in the mutually feigned reconciliation to prepare for the wedding masque is a winding down of dramatic tension.

That Middleton originally intended to do more with the play than this is clear, I think, from the second intrusion of the Cardinal. The Cardinal comes upon the pomp and worldly security of Bianca's wedding festivities, no longer merely as a vehicle of conscience, but as a projection of an absolute morality. As Alsemero weighs upon Beatrice in *The Changeling*, so the Cardinal weighs upon the Duke and his bride. Their marriage is no better defence against the consequences of sin than is the sanctuary of a 'privileged temple' to the convicted criminal, or the body to the sinner, since he knows that he must die.

> Man's only privileged temple upon earth
> In which the guilty soul takes sanctuary.
>
> [IV.3.43]

The passage looks back to Leantio's third image of the temple built upon rotting carcases and we know, though the Cardinal does not appear to, that one of the carcases is the body of Bianca's first husband.

This concept of the misused sanctuary, which is his retort to the Duke's excuse that he has taken the way to lawful love, is significantly placed after the seductions and contrivances of previous scenes. But Bianca's reply is too emphatic to be ignored. For Bianca the Cardinal's uncompromising righteousness lacks the charity which as Heaven's 'servant' he should profess. To the lost, the inwardly blind, it can do 'no wrong' (and presumably, no good), but for the penitent it takes away the 'light from one that

sees', and she continues to adapt the temple image with the idea
of reconstruction:

> 'Tis nothing virtue's temples to deface;
> But build the ruins, there's a work of grace.

[IV.3.68]

The defaced temple of the human spirit we shall recognise later in
Bianca's 'blemished face', stained with the poison she has drunk,
which to her externalises a spiritual ruin.

> But my deformity in spirit's more foul;
> A blemished face best fits a leprous soul.

[V.2.202]

This highly imaginative, if undramatic debate clarifies what
Middleton probably intended by the play as a whole. Bianca's
argument for the more liberal training of girls, Isabella's strictures
on the state of marriage, the exposure of the subjection of women,
have all been leading up to this final plea for the restoration of a
human life when it falls into self-destruction. We know that the
plea must fail, for behind the Cardinal is the evidence in history
of the laws that govern human existence, but between the irre-
concilables of Livia's savage denunciation and Bianca's searching
criticism of moral absolutism lies the new, but as yet only partially
realised, tragic view of life towards which Middleton was moving.
But retribution and reconstruction cannot be contained in the
same play. Moreover the Cardinal's moral function is so far
removed in spirit from the events of the previous scene that the
two plots which have hitherto developed in harmony, now part
company with disconcerting suddenness. We encounter the Cardinal as the voice of Tiresias or the oracle of Apollo. Livia's
revelation has something of the ferocity of the scene of Gloucester's
blinding in *King Lear*, and the tragic effect arises from the stark-
ness of plain fact. The Cardinal's judgment belongs to classical
tragedy, Livia's retribution has its basis in the ruthless objectivity
of comedy, and the artifice of the final scene will not fuse them.
After the destruction of love between Isabella and Hippolyto
Bianca's appeal has no relevance, or perhaps their situation
demanded a different kind of resolution which Middleton's
sources could not provide.

The fact is that we see Middleton here for the first time

defeated by disparate material. Bianca's story—a historical story at that, with which only certain liberties might be taken—was a natural vehicle for traditional tragedy. Beatrice could murder at second-hand and remain credible in her sheer muddle-headedness, but it is difficult to accept the same crime first-hand from Bianca as Middleton handles her without a further phase of development. It is possible that Middleton originally intended only one entrance by the Cardinal, for the removal of Leantio is a sufficiently ironic comment on the efficacy of his first one. As it is, the Cardinal's second appearance retards the action and the mechanical use of symbolism in the wedding masque dissipates the effect of climax. Livia is no doubt aptly presented as Juno Pro-nuba— the celestial bawd—but Bianca's end has been ill prepared for.

Mr. Schoenbaum draws attention to the presence of moral exponents in Middleton's later comedies.[9] But the moralists of the comedies are in a different category from those in the tragedies. Like Livia they are of the plot and speak to characters of their own level.[10] In this play the frank resort to polemic, the urge to preach and explain, are new to Middleton. But so also is the deliberate and, as we have seen, often highly successful use of image sequences, such as the recurrence of Leantio's temple image, on which the action is frequently built; and of symbolism —or images so placed as to function as symbols—like that of the chess game. Throughout the impression is of an anxious care to make the most of the material, to develop character and meaning with all the artistry experience had brought.

Once more Middeton's habitual restraint is at work. He had seen the possibilities of tragedy in the commonplaces of life, and the discipline of satirical comedy had strengthened his powers in the objective study of human personality. But even in *The Changeling* we know the characters mainly from without. In *Women Beware Women* soliloquy, asides, confidences with the audience are aids to the unravelling of motive on a deeper level, but the themes the play poses can be adequately presented only from within the minds of the characters. In contrast to the vivid figures of Jacobean tragedy Middleton's characters, though drawn with disturbing realism, are still conceived without intensity. It is this lack of intensity within the characters that makes catharsis impossible; hence perhaps his frequent failure in denouement. Basically Middleton's interest is neither in purgation nor repentance as such, but rather in the contrast between men's aspirations and their human fallibility. It was this endemic moral and spiritual immaturity in average people that caught his attention as a dramatist; it was the source of his comic irony and its closer scrutiny led to the writing of tragedy. Thus the emphasis in Middleton's tragedies is on discovery and reversal, but it is not pity that he asks of us but rather recognition of the human capacity for suffering which in itself confers a kind of dignity. Unfortunately in this his last tragedy, the attempt to widen his scope carried him to limits beyond which his only recourse was to moral statement; this, however impressive, was to substitute philosophic poetry for living drama.

So *Women Beware Women* is an experiment which partly fails, especially in the last Act; yet the play as a whole is some indication of what Middleton intended to do with serious drama. His use in tragedy of a plot activated by one character playing upon the frailty of another, tentatively suggested in the main plot of *A Fair Quarrel*, was an instinctive step in his development. For it provided opportunity for the realism in dialogue and background which makes the reading and acting of this play a continually fresh experience. The total effect upon an audience is of an intimacy with the characters which makes their contrarieties acceptable.

Middleton's obvious innovation is of a new type of tragic hero in the figure of Leantio, with his capacity for depth of feeling and his aspirations balanced against his limitations and innate vulgarity. To make such a character credible and to keep him in his proper place within the pattern of the play was no mean achievement. And the women characters are made up of similarly disparate elements. The post-Restoration qualities often noted in Middleton can be seen, surprisingly, here. The Bianca of the middle Acts, her aspirations to 'fashion'—how often is the word on her lips!—the hard sparkling wit of her replies at the banquet, the coldness of her taunts to Leantio, would not be out of place in Congreve. Yet the same character is brought to the limits of mortality before the play closes, and this without violence to that hard consistency of character which anticipates later seventeenth-century comedy.

In all this the influence of Webster, whose own modifications to the pattern of Revenge Tragedy in his two greatest plays made such an impact on the theatre, should not be ruled out. It is possible that Webster's tragi-comedy *The Devil's Law Case*, with its social implications, its substitution of the merchant for the prince as hero, was in Middleton's mind. At the same time it is illuminating to compare Webster's final comment (on the Cardinal) in *The Duchess of Malfi* with Middleton's summary, in Hippolyto's words, towards the end of *Women Beware Women*:

> . . . thou which stood'st like a huge Piramid
> Begun upon a large and ample base,
> Shalt end in a little point, a kind of nothing.
> > [*Duchess of Malfi*. V.5.96]

> Lust and forgetfulness have been among us
> And we are brought to nothing.
> > [*Women Beware Women*. V.1.187]

The difference is that between their respective views of tragedy. Webster's Cardinal has grown upwards in pride and prosperity from a basis of power and aggrandisement. The image is concrete and strongly visual, and the wording from 'huge', 'large and ample', to the phrase 'a little point', 'a kind of nothing' has a diminishing effect, emotionally the stronger for its logical aptness. Webster's intention is to demonstrate, irrespective of desert, the horrifying inevitability of the great man's fall. In contrast Middleton clarifies his thought by the skilful placing of a single word. 'Forgetfulness' is sufficiently matter-of-fact, but here in association with 'lust' it sets up a kaleidoscope of meaning. Bianca's wilfulness, Leantio's unconsidered haste, Livia's undisciplined affection, Isabella's irresponsibility, the easy morals of the Duke and Hippolyto, are brought up sharply against the fact of lust which the Ward embodies but which informs them all. Such emotional overtones as there are—and of course much depends upon the actor—are directed by a single word so much towards the consequences of action that the final 'nothing' falls, not with a sense of catastrophe but with an impression of judgment.

This summary treatment of the idea of retributive justice, the basic theme of Revenge Tragedy, typifies Middeton's attitude to the theatre of his day. The spectacle of Macbeth reaping the reward of his crimes is a major interest in the plot of Shakespeare's play, but the drama also emphasises both the significance of his career in the wider context of the State and the greatness of his fall from what he might have been. The destruction of that which might have 'proved most royally' is as recurrent in Elizabethan tragedy as the 'horror' that waits upon the death of princes in the Jacobean theatre; and beyond the death of the tragic character is 'the undiscovered country' or the workings of an inscrutable providence in the course of history. Whether deserved or not the fall of the hero confronts us with a mysterious universe in which man is at least important enough for the gods to punish. With Middleton the tragic experience turns upon the logic of consequences worked out in the small circle of human intercourse. The effect is achieved not by building on the feelings, but by controlling and containing them. The play closes not upon a heroic failure, not on a character ennobled or strengthened by suffering, nor with the visitation of destiny upon one outstanding figure, but on a group of inter-related and essentially undistinguished people who after their dreams and evasions are returned to their proper level. The uniqueness of *Women Beware Women* is in the attempt in the final scenes to balance the irony of the characters' recognition of their true deserts against a moral law no less incongruous to their human condition than the illusions which have destroyed them.

In all this we may distinguish the attitude and artifice of comedy. For tragic intensity Middleton substitutes tensions within the characters which, though often generated by circumstances, are moral in the long run. Like the majority of mankind they are people of good intention, with motives rather confused than mixed. It is the character of comic stature brought up against an acute psychological or moral challenge—the challenge faced by Beatrice on her wedding night or by Bianca as she sees her bridegroom die at her own hands—that gives to Middleton's tragedy its characteristic edge. One is driven to the conclusion that the violence of the closing scenes of the two tragedies is largely a concession to a mode. With Middleton there are no heights or depths in the passions of the flesh, only a retardation of the spirit which it takes the reversals of life, not an encounter with the universal mysteries in death, to cure. Thus at the catastrophe there is nothing to regret, nothing to condemn or admire, only a good deal to understand.

The concluding aphorism in *Women Beware Women* is a suitable comment on his thinking in tragedy to date:

> . . . man's understanding
> Is riper at his fall than all his lifetime.

[V.I.193]

Of Middleton's characters it may be truly said that they 'come'
to understanding and the lesson is not the less impressive because
they are slow to learn it. That the impact of the two tragedies is as
sharp and fresh today as it probably was when they were first
acted is some proof that he was moving in the right direction. He
had shown that tragic drama could be written without the traditional formulae; it was unfortunate that he had no time to
develop the discovery in a more perfect play than *Women Beware
Women*. In the event a combination of circumstances in the world
outside the theatre, coinciding perhaps with some situation arising
within it, diverted his attenion to political satire in *A Game at
Chess*.

6.   *A Game at Chess*

> What a pain it is
> For truth to feign a little!

WHATEVER the play's value as satire, this is a major theme in *A Game at Chess*. Where simple honesty and plain falsehood fail equivocation may succeed; dissimulation can be counteracted only by dissimulation. This is the drama of what Middleton calls in the Prologue 'fallacy',[1] the chicanery which had occupied his imagination through many years of work for the stage and which his more recent experience had shaped into a representation of human behaviour. If *A Game at Chess* cut short his revaluation of Jacobean tragedy it carried a stage further the opposition of truth and falsehood which was the theme of *A Fair Quarrel* and a major interest in *The Changeling* and *Women Beware Women*.

The play's general quality is astonishing considering the speed with which it must have been written. May 13th, 1624 saw the conclusion of the trial and impeachment of the Earl of Middlesex. Middlesex had already made himself unpopular in supporting the proposals for the marriage between Prince Charles and the Spanish Infanta four years previously, and now the continual dread of pro-Roman Catholic policy in England and above all, of a possible alliance with Spain, inflamed a good deal of public interest in the proceedings against him. Within a month *A Game at Chess* was completed, so that if R. C. Bald is right in identifying the turncoat White King's Pawn with Middlesex,[2] this trial was the immediate occasion of the play.

Both before and after the fall of Middlesex, Middleton evidently read all he could find—tracts, pamphlets, letters—that bore on the conduct of Catholics in England; that much of what he read was biased, that what he could imbibe from it in the short time at his disposal was less actual fact than the popular interpretation of events, only aided his purpose. On June 12th the play was licensed by Sir Henry Herbert; it was first performed by the King's Men on August 6th[3] and ran for the then unprecedented extent of nine consecutive days. Crowds swarmed to the Globe, people of all classes saw and talked of the play and scrambled for places on the hard benches of the theatre, where they sat for more than an hour before a performance began. Then, after August 16th, the authorities acted; the play was prohibited and the theatre closed during the King's pleasure. With characteristic astuteness Middleton temporarily disappeared, though there are grounds for supposing that he was imprisoned for a short period. When his son represented him before the Council the players protested their innocence with some justification, for after all, in spite of its implication, the play had been licensed for performance. But whatever the inconvenience they suffered, and it was probably little more, the sensation which the play created was not forgotten, and no doubt what was loss to the theatre was gain for the printer, for it was published after a surprisingly short interval —in 1625, according to the date on the title page of the second Quarto. Equally surprising is the reproduction on the title page of all three Quartos of the figures, from well known portraits, of the two main targets in the political satire—Gondamar, the Spanish Ambassador and De Dominis, Archbishop of Spalatro, as the Black Knight and the Fat Bishop.[4]

When in 1623 Prince Charles and the Duke of Buckingham returned from Spain without a prospective bride—an incident which Middleton records as the return of the White Knight and Duke from their visit to the Black House, whence they are welcomed 'with loud peals of joy'—the sinister power of Gondamar over the mind and policy of the King seemed eclipsed. Lewd jokes about the fistula from which he suffered, reference to his litter and chair of ease, were in constant circulation. The chair and litter were sketched on the title page of the anti-Catholic tract *Vox Populi*, Part II, which appeared in the following year, and both were actually reproduced on the stage in Middleton's play; it was even rumoured that the costume for the actor who played the Black Knight was a suit once worn by Gondamar himself.[5] He was food for popular farce as well as political satire, and an obvious choice as a major character for a dramatist with a feeling for what a popular audience liked. And there were plenty of supporting characters—Philip IV himself as the Black King, Olivares the Spanish Chief Minister as the Black Duke and, most important, De Dominis as the Fat Bishop.

De Dominis had long since turned from the narrow teaching of the Jesuits to seek a broader religious outlook; he had eventually become Archbishop of Spalatro and had then sought an outlet for his more moderate views by courting the King's favour in England. Like all those who seek a middle way in a period of controversy, De Dominis seemed to those who did not know him a time-pleaser and turncoat. In fact he was an unfortunate who found rest nowhere, and when in 1622 he resolved to return to Italy on the accession of Pope Gregory XV who had been his friend in the past, the latter died within the year, leaving De Dominis to failure and isolation. But to Protestant middle-class England De Dominis was a figure of fun; his obesity was sufficient outward evidence of greed and the writings in which he had tried to justify his position, as well as the steps he had taken to preserve his possessions on leaving the country, all seemed to underline the self-assurance with which he had looked for honours while he had the King's confidence.

All this evidently crowded up into Middleton's mind at the fall of Middlesex, who like De Dominis had enjoyed the favour of King James, the White King of the play. As De Dominis in religion, Middlesex had tried to find a moderate way in policy; Middleton presents him as the turncoat White King's Pawn, black within though white without, a smaller version of the Fat Bishop.[6] But behind the political figures lie the popular idea of Jesuit practice, rumours of abuse of the monastic rule in religious houses, the scandals connected with private lives of celibate priests and professed nuns, the intrigues of Jesuit fathers both in the habit and in secular disguise, superstitious practices and equivocal teaching on the vow of obedience, the sale of indulgences and the abuse of the confessional, and finally the dread of Jesuit schemes for universal indoctrination. All this is projected in the symbolic figures of the Black and White Queens, the rival churches, with their attendant embodiments of lust and innocence respectively, in the Black and White Queens' Pawns.

At first sight, Middleton's dramatic material seems to fall into the pattern of his characteristic work. The black and white chessmen represent the Catholic and Protestant parties, but they carry certain moral distinctions, clarified as the play opens, through the minor 'pieces' whose story is Middleton's invention. In the White Queen's Pawn we have again the unsophisticated girl, ready prey

for the worldly contriving woman, the 'bouncing Jesuitess' who
is the Black Queen's Pawn, her opposite number in the game as in
the moral values for which she stands. In the opening scene the
Black Queen's Pawn attempts to inveigle her into the Black
House, but this missionary zeal is the cover for a more sinister
design—to betray her, much as Isabella is betrayed by Livia, to
the lust of the Jesuit Black Bishop's Pawn, whose whim she
indulges out of a secret desire to enjoy him herself. Once more
we have the natural bawd plying her business under cover of
kindly intention, while the White Queen's Pawn's disillusionment
and resistance may derive from the predicament of Jane in *A Fair
Quarrel*.

Thus in his role of confessor, the Black Bishop's Pawn makes
his first assault; when persuasion fails and he attempts a rape, the
Black Queen's Pawn is there again, resourceful as ever, to save
him from committing an outrage which would have defeated both
their purposes. In a trial scene in which both Houses appear, the
White Queen's Pawn is convicted on false evidence of slander,
but is afterwards vindicated by the timely intervention of the
White Knight; whereupon the Black Queen's Pawn proceeds to
win her confidence afresh by the supposed vision of a destined
husband in the magic glass. This is however none other than the
would-be seducer, disguised, after the manner of missionary
Jesuits, in rich worldly attire. After persuading the dazzled girl to
lie with him on the pretence of a pre-contract, he is tricked in
turn by the Black Queen's Pawn, who substitutes herself under
cover of darkness—much as Alsemero is tricked by Diaphanta,
the substitute bride of *The Changeling*. Thus, as in Middleton's
comedies, the trickster is tricked and innocence preserved.

There is however a secondary theme. The White Queen's
Pawn has a true lover, the White Bishop's Pawn, who has suffered castration at the hands of his jealous rival, the Black
Knight's Pawn. The latter's 'tender-hoof'd' conscience, sharply
contrasted with the cynicism of the Black Knight and the Fat
Bishop, to whom he turns in remorse for penance and pardon, is
presented with a deliberation that recalls the scruples of Captain
Ager and the uneasiness of De Flores. The theme of conscience
has its interest for Middleton in other connections, but nowhere
else has he space to elaborate it as here, where it occupies a
considerable part of the action.

These are the concerns of the politically less important figures; but behind them is the immense machine of policy, with its artists in double-dealing, conceived on a larger scale than in any of Middleton's previous studies in chicanery. His evident intention was to utilise every available link between the real Gondamar and De Dominis so as to make a broad attack on the policy of both Church and State. The Black Knight, bending the ambitions of lesser men to the shape of his own vested interests in the 'universal monarchy' of the (Catholic) Black House, is the exponent of dishonest statecraft, while the Fat Bishop, his inveterate rival, is an ecclesiastical freebooter, seeking his advantage wherever it may be found, changing sides as readily as the lesser intriguer, the Black Bishop's Pawn, his disguises. Inevitably the astute politician wins, entangling the Fat Bishop in a recantation, on the promise of promotion contained in a faked letter from his supposed 'princely kinsman' in Rome.[7] It is however the White Bishop (Archbishop Abbot) who brings the White King on the scene to beat him 'into the bag' on surprising him in an attempt to take possession of the White Queen. The incident reflects De Dominis's presumptuous effort to persuade King James to grant him the Archbishopric of York, for there is a subtle reference to this climax of his ambitious schemes in the Fat Bishop's lines:

> Then for their sanctimonious Queen's surprisal . . .
> Trust my *Arch* subtlety with.
>
> [IV.2.141–3]

on which the Black Knight comments: 'Oh eagle pride!'

Finally the Back Knight, with the rest of the Black House, meets his deserts when the White Knight, with the White Duke in attendance, checkmates the Black side by evoking from them a confession of dissembling.

I can add nothing to R. C. Bald's summary of Middleton's probable sources. Sharp as is the attack, it is clear that the prejudice exists in what Middleton was drawing upon and not only in himself, and the swift selection with which he worked, the mass of material which he absorbed into his purpose, can scarcely be rivalled even in Shakespeare. His dramatic instinct seizes jackdaw-like on any detail to illumine the plot. Gondamar's disease is pin-pointed in the pregnant phrase 'the fistula of Europe' (II.2.45); his litter and chair of ease are not only brought upon the stage, they are referred to in the text. Fuller's delightful description of De Dominis as 'somewhat abdominous and corpulent in body'[8] could recall another phrase from *Spalatro's Doome* of 1624, which Middleton had probably read—'the titular Dalmatian Bishop who before like another Leviathan would drink up Jordan, and overthrow the Pope's Supremacie.'[9] These impressions are suggested in the rolling syllables of the Fat Bishop's own lines:

> I'd have some round preferment, corpulent dignity,
> That bears some breadth and comfort in the gift on't:
> I am persuaded that this flesh would fill
> The biggest chair ecclesiastical,
> If it were put to trial.
>
> [III.1.7]

Middleton may well have written this play in haste, his desk scattered with such tracts as Robinson's *Anatomie of the English Nunnerie at Lisbon* of 1622, *The Frier's Chronicle* of the same year, John Gee's *Foot out of the Snare*, and Reynolds's *Vox Coeli*, of 1624, with the two parts of the *Vox Populi*, both by Scott, on which he drew most freely. Yet although a good deal is repeated from the text, his modifications of his sources are often startling. For instance the excuse quoted in *The Frier's Chronicle* for the priest seen kissing a woman—'You must suppose he did it to imprint a blessing on her lips'—is Middleton's hint for the Black Bishop's Pawn's equivocal wooing of the White Queen's Pawn.

> If I can at that distance send you a blessing,
> Is it not nearer to you in mine arms?
> It flies from these lips dealt abroad in parcels.
>
> [II.1.67]

And Robinson's comment that the Jesuits will cherish their converts 'in their own bosoms' receives a lascivious twist in the Black Queen's Pawn's addition of 'tractable sweet obedient' and the repetitive phrase 'in his own dear bosom' in:

> . . . so will he cherish
> All his young, tractable, sweet, obedient daughters
> In his own bosom, in his own dear bosom.
>
> [I.1.38]

Again, the comparison of the Jesuit adventurers to locusts swarming in 'disordered orders', develops in Middleton's hands into the Black Knight's realistic image of the locusts invading the country crops and sticking

> . . . so fast to the converted ears
> The loudest tempest that Authority rouses
> Will hardly shake 'em off.
>
> [III.1.97]

—and the comment attributed to Gondamar in the first part of *Vox Populi*, that certain time-servers will 'milk the estate and keep it poor' takes on new life in the same character's self-congratulatory statement:

> The Court has held the City by the horns
> While I have milk'd her.
>
> [III.1.108]

In every case Middleton turns a straightforward prose statement into a description of double-dealing as witty as it is vivid. It is here that he breaks new ground; the skill acquired in earlier experiments in dramatic irony in *A Chaste Maid in Cheapside* and *The Changeling* is now focused upon the theme of equivocation, which he had touched upon at the comic level in *A Trick to Catch the Old One*. The greatest equivocator is naturally the politician himself, the Black Knight-Gondamar who, according to the White Duke, will 'teach the devil how to lie'. In his own words he 'will change to any shape To please you', and it is he who recommends the rash and lust-driven Black King to take the way of indirection:

> BL. KING: That Queen would I fain finger.
> BL. KNIGHT: You're too hot, sir,
> If she were took, the game would be ours
>   quickly;
> My aim's at that white Knight, entrap him first
> The Duke will follow too.
>
> [III.1.244]

The cunning with which he lures the White King's Pawn into the net with promises of promotion reflects the craft of the machiavel.

> A staff
> That will not easily break; you may trust to't;
> (Aside) And such a one had your corruption need of.
>
> [II.2.220]

But it is through the underlings, equivocators no less skilful than he, that Middleton's attack involves the Jesuitical system as a whole. The scenes between the White Queen's Pawn and her two assailants, the Black Queen's and the Black Bishop's Pawns, are built up almost entirely on two levels of meaning. The seducer bases his first attempt on the equivocal nature of the vow of obedience, and the subsequent pre-contract is a similarly fallacious quibble. At his first entrance the Black Queen's Pawn announces him as one before whom Princes will fall prostrate, adding significantly, 'Women are weaker vessels'. His teaching on the confessional has the same barely concealed implication.

> The privat'st thought that runs to hide itself
> In the most secret corner of your heart now,
> Must be of my acquaintance, so familiarly
> Never she-friend of your night-counsels nearer.
>
> [I.1.123]

Finally it is the Black Knight's praise of dissembling as the weapon of his side in general that causes the downfall of the Black House, the home and centre of Jesuitism, 'check-mate by discovery'.

It was not unnatural that Middleton who like some of his contemporaries had used the game of chess to build up suspense, by preoccupying or distracting the victim of deception while taking the audience into his confidence, should conceive it now as a figure of chicanery. His faithfulness to the conception is worth noting; all the characters, like those in 'Alice Through the Looking-Glass', are in the game. References to moves in the game are constant and carefully calculated; the pawn defends the queen, to take the queen is as good as to win the game, and risks are taken with the important white pieces, the Knight and the Duke (or rook), in order to checkmate the Black side. The 'round-about' movement of the knight on the chess-board has a certain suitability as representing the counter-intrigues of the rival political leaders, Gondamar and Prince Charles, knights

in the game.[10] Meantime the 'bag' which Middleton identifies
with the Hell-mouth of the Mystery Plays, waits to swallow up
the fallen chess-men. But the game is evil in itself; it is engineered
by Ignatius with the help of Error, the aggressive moves are all
on the part of the Black House, the White merely playing for
resistance, until the final move which is undertaken, it should be
noted, to the distress of the White Queen. If the White Queen
represents the Reformed Church, her concern for the White
Knight's safety and the White King's half rebuking reassurance
must have had an interesting implication for a London audience
still smarting under the threat of a marriage pact with Spain.
But the one-sidedness of the 'game' and the White Pawn's final
repudiation both of her lover and her would-be seducer, carry
Middleton's satire beyond its immediate political significance.

This may partly explain the unusual balance of the two aspects
of the plot. Whatever the speed with which Middleton amassed
his material when the opportunity for political satire presented
itself, it seems likely that he had been reading and considering
his sources for some time previously; that he had perhaps stored
in his mind the idea of the corrupt professor and the innocent,
not so tractable girl, not necessarily as having any immediate
significance, until the events of 1623–4 drew his thinking into
a particular channel. It is a mistake to regard the pawns' story
as a secondary plot; indeed both plots are introduced and
attention emphatically drawn to that of the pawns, in the
Prologue spoken by Ignatius, and the action involving the pawns
sets a good deal of the rest of the play in motion. In the opening
scene the attack upon the White Pawn's virtue begins and we
also hear of her lover and his rival who provide a secondary
theme. It is the seducer's failure that draws the Black Knight
into the plot, since not only the 'great work stands' but the
Black House also suffers in reputation with him. Thenceforward
the two plots are linked both politically and morally, the pawns
serving the intriguers in their efforts for 'the universal Monarchy',
all of which in twice involving the two Houses in trying her
cause are made to depend on the virtue of the White Queen's
Pawn.

At each turn of events the Black Knight is there to back the
lesser characters with his practical expedients. This consummate
plotter is nevertheless defeated in his ruse to cover the flight of

the Black Bishop's Pawn, but meantime he has begun his intrigue
against the Fat Bishop, so that when one piece of action has
begun to resolve itself another is under way. The involvement of
the Fat Bishop in the pawns' story, when the Black Knight brings
his own conscience-ridden pawn to consult with him the Taxa
Poenitentiaria, is another interesting development. Circumstantially the links are loose but the overall impression is one of unity.
This impression is strengthened by the White Knight's intervention in order to aid the innocent pawn and by his ultimate
assault upon the Black House in a deed of daring which is the
admiration of the White House and the confusion of the Black.
And meanwhile his enterprise is paralleled by the overthrow of
the Fat Bishop by the White King in defence of his Queen—a
delicate compliment to King James. It is a crescendo of excitement and significance planned with considerable constructional
skill. In so crowded a scene it would have been easy to leave some
ends untied, but every issue is resolved, every character con-
vincingly accounted for, and the overlapping of the various
phases of action holds the play together with a musical, fugal
effect.

The treatment of character is another balancing factor. The
pawns' plot is a complete narrative and we can live with the
characters in the course of it, although the political fable is
necessarily episodic. Middleton's skill in selecting characters for
development in the round keeps the interest even. The two main
political figures are fully drawn in a relationship which amounts
to a plot in embryo, with the Fat Bishop at the centre of an
intrigue which tempts him to overstep his prerogative and fall
in consequence. But the pawns, though more lightly sketched,
are no lay figures. The White Queen's Pawn is surely more than
'virtuous without being dull'.[11] With the untried potentiality
of Middleton's earlier heroines at the beginning of their stories,
she is at first only bewildered by the strange behaviour of those
in whom she trusts. Her refusal to judge or condemn even the
one who has destroyed her lover's manhood, is evidence less of a
pious than of an unspoilt nature. It is the same loyalty to herself
rather than to a code of morals that makes her impervious to
the Black Bishop's Pawn's equivocal arguments and finally
obdurate in resisting his assault. The artlessness with which she
yields to the pleasure of seeing her destined husband in the magic

glass is the same as that which prompts her description of herself as the orderly housewife of her own mind:

> So in the congregation of quick thoughts . . .
> I cannot with truth's safety speak for all:
> Some have been wanderers, some fond, some sinful,
> But these found ever but poor entertainment,
> They had small encouragement to come again.
>
> [I.1.133]

She has the child's integrity which turns evil suggestions into
good.

> By holiness of garment, her innocence
> Has frighted the full meaning from itself
>
> [II.1.42]

is the Black Pawn's comment when he vainly tempts her with thinly
veiled soliciting. The White Pawn is garbed in the innocence
which should have been his spiritual garment, but he is made to
encounter her rather as an unfamiliar human problem than as
an embodied virtue armed against his attack. There is no barrenness in her chastity; she is excited like any girl on Hallowe'en at
the promised vision of her lover, still eager to enjoy him lawfully
notwithstanding her vehement rebuke of his impatience when
she meets him in the flesh. Yet she is poor material for the Jesuit's
confessional, not because of her perfection, but because she
knows no sins that would be to his purpose and because her
natural integrity makes her unable to fabricate any to oblige him.
This, perhaps the most delicate of Middleton's conceptions, is
executed with a lyricism which, as we shall see, Milton may have
been consciously recalling in the Lady of *Comus*.

For contrast the White Queen's Pawn is set against the older
woman—like Livia, experienced in prurience; and like Livia,
though without her geniality, the Black Queen's Pawn is half
in love with the seducer she aids, and when all fails it is with
something of Livia's ruthlessness that she turns upon her
accomplice. That Livia was in Middleton's mind seems likely
from the lines in which she vindicates herself:

> . . . pray, look upon me, sir,
> I've youth enough to take it[12]
>
> [V.2.95]

—and like Livia she excels in that managing ability and quick resource which leave her unabashed even when disaster overtakes her.

The seducer himself is still more finely drawn; to whatever depths he falls the Black Bishop's Pawn is never less than a Jesuit father. His approach is tactful and courteous; it is only when his intended victim's invulnerability proves more than he had bargained for that he begins to lose control both of his art and of his passions. To fall in love was no part of his purpose, and the unexpected drives him beyond the limits of his prudence.

> I never was so taken; beset doubly
> Now with her judgment.
>
> [I.1.174]

It is not solely Jesuit hypocrisy that Middleton's satire unveils; it is also the haplessness of the practitioner, reared on a system, encountering an unfamiliar set of values. With a characteristic touch of comedy, Middleton exposes him to a yet more grievous shock when at their second meeting the girl, with the logic of youth, proves quite impervious to the appeal of his own predicament now that he is committed beyond withdrawal. Rape is his last resource—not his intention—and the Black Queen's Pawn saves him in the nick of time. At heart he is the simplest character in the play, easy game for the lively Jesuitess who plans all his moves and whose understanding of character, like Livia's comprehension of Isabella in a not dissimilar situation, actuates the cleverly prepared ruse of the pre-contract.

Finally, there is the helpless penitent—the Black Knight's Pawn—appalled at the nature of his crime, bewildered at the worldly imperturbability of his ghostly fathers, high placed and reverend as they are, and driven by moral shock into worse offence still. Here is a rich store of dramatic material, fertile in human situation, and it is no small credit to Middleton's control of his creative impulse that he can subordinate it to a satirical purpose. For convincing as they are, these characters are two-dimensional; they are etched merely, and we see them only from without. The White Queen's Pawn passes through the play like a musical theme and some of Middleton's most lyrical passages are spoken by her or addressed to her by the other characters in her story; yet she and they are nameless and without a single personal detail which might identify them or relate them to a recognisable living figure. Nor do we sense with them, as we do with Beatrice-Joanna or De Flores, the disarranged and tormented nature of human beings in the wear and tear of ordinary life. They are living types but they remain types; fertile as their story is in realistic comment, it occupies only half our attention.

On the other hand the political aspect of the play is based on little plot as such, but it presents the two dominant figures, the Black Knight and the Fat Bishop, whom it was necessary to make immediately recognisable. The background figures in the chess game are no more than puppets. The two Queens are symbols, the two Kings are identified by their associates within the plot—and of course by their costume—and the White King's Pawn makes his presence felt only by the conundrum he presents to the commentator. The Black Bishop is identified in the text as the Father General (I.1.49–50), and the White Bishop may, as has been suggested, represent Abbot, but either character could, on grounds of personality, be identified as easily with anyone else. But whether fairly or not, Gondamar and De Dominis are drawn to the life.

From the first words he speaks Gondamar is an individual, and we sense his cold sardonic nature in his unimpassioned dismissal of any concern that contributes nothing to his own schemes:

> The business of the Universal Monarchy
> Goes forward well now, the great College pot
> That should be always boiling . . .
>   Is this fellow
> Our prime incendiary? . . .
>   Put a new daughter to him
> The great work stands.
>
>   [I.1.243]

His reverence towards his Confessor is open parody—

> BL. B.P.: Blessings' accumulation keep with you, Sir.
> BL. KT.: Honour's dissimulation be your due, Sir.
>
>   [I.1.271]

There is nothing that he cannot accurately evaluate save virtue, which for him does not exist; 'So, is your trifle vanish't?' is his sole recognition of the White Queen's Pawn. But the Black Knight understands the game and his lively intelligence relishes policy for its own sake; when the 'bouncing Jesuitess' makes a last attempt to corrupt the White Pawn by flattery (on the discovery of the plot against her), he alone can appreciate the 'master-piece of roguery' which 'this drum strikes up for'. Yet he under-stands himself with no less ironic detachment; beneath his suave courtesy he is aware of his own cruelty as he is aware of his physical disease, and in asserting his mastery of intrigue—plots to the number of 'twelve thousand and nine hundred fourscore and five'—with, as foil, his penitent, yet half envious Pawn, he revives the machiavel in a new guise.

In depicting yet another machiavel before a public theatre audience in 1624, Middleton was taking certain risks. The bogey politician of Jacobean tragedy, with his tortuous brain and his schemes veiled in the mystery of a superhuman intelligence, had had his day. Even Webster, for whom the machiavel had a lasting fascination, had applied cool reason to the conception in his Romelio and in his Appius in and after 1620.[13] But Middleton's conception of Gondamar unites some of the qualities of the traditional machiavel with the business acumen of the successful merchant. His own account of his villainies recalls the machin-ations of the politician skilled in handling the minds of men:

> To many a soul I've let in mortal poison
> Whose cheeks have crack'd with laughter to receive it;
> I could so roll my pills in sugar'd syllables,
> And strew such kindly mirth o'er all my mischief,
> They took their bane in way of recreation,
> As pleasure steals corruption into youth.
>
> 　　　　　　　　　　　　　　　　[I.1.261]

His complacency in taking stock has an affinity with Romelio's worldly-wise ambition to assume the guise of a 'rare Italianated Jew'.

> To winde about a man like rotten Ivie,
> Eate into him like Quicksilver, poyson a friend . . .
> With pulling out a loose hair from's beard, or give a drench
> He should linger of't nine yeares and nere complain . . .
> 　　　　　　　. . . for sleight villanies,
> As to coyne money, corrupt Ladies Honours,

> Betray a Towne to the Turke, or make a Bonefire
> A'th Christiane Navy, I could settle to't
> As if I had eate a Politician
> And digested him to nothing but pure blood.[14]

But the Black Knight successfully is what Romelio tries, and fails, to be; he has no inner conflict, nor is he a spider at the centre of a web of policy, intricate though his schemes may be. He bustles in the foreground of the political scene; his craft is complicated not mysterious, and while he is no Cecil we must, with his bewildered Pawn, credit him with some stature on his own level. For in the Black Knight's scheme of values, a man is great in proportion to the 'swallow of his conscience'. He is comic in his absolute consistency; in his rich self-satisfaction at both his cleverness and his crimes, his suave claim to absolute wickedness, he assumes the very spirit of sardonic laughter. Where Marlowe would have given us a Jew of Malta, the Black Knight's 'swapping sins' and multiplicity of plots place him in the category of what Herbert Spencer would have termed 'descending incongruity', but without a trace of abashment or belittlement. From his safe eminence, the world is a joke and himself the best joke in it—'My light spleen skips and shakes my ribs to think on't'—and when he over-reaches himself, Middleton wisely gives him nothing to say. To make the machiavel a tragic figure was comparatively easy; to use him without losing the sense of his power as a figure of satirical comedy was a more difficult achievement.

No better contrast could be found than the Fat Bishop. Seizing upon the notorious ambition and arrogance of De Dominis, Middleton has reconstructed the figure of the eternal clown. Like the Black Bishop's Pawn, in contrast to the Black Queen's Pawn, the Fat Bishop is a simpleton at heart, and in making him caricature himself Middleton extracts the last ounce of fun both from what was popularly assumed of De Dominis himself, and from what was traditionally expected of the clown. The Black Knight's phrase—'balloon ball'—aptly describes him; his very words rollick, and the phrases he applies to himself limn his character with an almost visual effect:

> For great I grant you, but greatly holy,
> There the soil alters: fat cathedral bodies

> Have very often but lean little souls . . .
> Like those big-bellied mountains.
>
> [II.2.3]

With unctuous relish he commends the White House 'for plenty and variety of victuals', and there is a wry wit in the lascivious twist which he gives to De Dominis's appointment as Master of the Savoy:

> I grant I live at ease, for I am made
> The master of the beds, the long acre of beds,
> But there's no Marygold that shuts and opens . . .
> There was a time I had more drabs than beds,
> Now I've more beds than drabs.
>
> [II.2.34]

His jokes upon himself are no more and no less offensive than his recommendation of the public hangman as a cure for the fistula, which earns him the enmity of the Black Knight-Gondamar. There is a certain ingenuousness in the vanity he displays under the latter's pitiless observation, as he reads the feigned letter:

> 'Right reverend and noble',—meaning ourself,—
>
> [III.1.33]

—and in his concern for the dignity of his 'episcopal person'. Yet it is he himself and not his enemy who describes his own confusion that will

> . . . let forth a Fat Bishop in sad syrop.
>
> [III.1.71]

Like all Middleton's major figures he preserves both his character and his sense of comedy when disaster overtakes him, scorning to 'stir for any King on earth', but (with a hint of caricature) when the Queen arrives,

> Indeed a Queen may make a Bishop stir.
>
> [V.3.199]

This overt enjoyment of his own grossness has a Falstaffian touch; it is after the manner of the stage clown, whose chief stock-in-trade is himself, and whose privilege lasts until he oversteps the bounds of prudence. The Fat Bishop is one who knows himself only as far as his self-esteem permits, and who is there-

fore easy game for the equally unscrupulous, but far more
disciplined, courtier and diplomat.

The satirical potentialities of this figure seem to owe no less
to his affinity with Ignatius in the Induction than to the parallel
with his original. Ignatius expresses the same dissatisfaction with
the honours done him:

> Where slept my honour all this time before?
> Could they be so forgetful to canonise
> Their prosperous Institutor
>
> [*Induction*: 16]

—and the same snobbishness, in his scorn of mere pawns that

> . . . argue but poor spirits and slight preferments.
>
> [*Induction*: 62]

Like the Fat Bishop when in the bag, his continual cry is for
more room in the Calendar. If attention were drawn to this
parallel in production—as it probably was—the behaviour of
the Fat Bishop would seem to ridicule not only De Dominis
himself, but the whole Jesuit hierarchy.

In thus making the characters reveal themselves from within,
Middleton gives his satire a double edge. What is castigated is
also humanised; there is no gnashing of the teeth to make us
doubt the author's sincerity. But Middleton's practised eye for
the dramatic situation within the contemporary problem sometimes leads him into risky double thrusts. So intent is he on
endowing all the leading personages with an individual voice
that even the Black King comes to life with his rankling wish:
'That Queen would I fain finger' (III.1.244). The significant
word is 'finger', with its suggestions of political greed and destructive power. Unfortunately it also stamps the otherwise un-
developed figure of the Black King with a lasciviousness which
might have cost his creator dear.[15]

To a dramatist with Middleton's powers of observation satire
was not enough. In making the Aunt Sallies assume a life of
their own he subordinates them to a set of moral and human
issues which goes deeper than his broad attack on the hypocrisy
which he seems to identify with Catholic policy. In the words
of the White Queen's Pawn at her trial, the Black House is
the house of 'impudence, Craft and equivocation', but in the
same scene she refers specifically to their opposites in the White

House—'noble candour, uncorrupted justice'—and, above all, 'truth of heart' (II.2.115–16, 194). In contrast the Black House has 'a treasure' in the 'false heart' of the renegade White King's Pawn. The White King is the 'King of integrity', the White Knight is 'truth's glorious master-piece', and it is as embodiments of integrity that he and his assistant Duke are acclaimed on their return. This can hardly be dismissed as flattery of the Court of King James; throughout the action integrity is posed against dissembling and it is this quality that comes to the aid of the White Queen's Pawn to triumph over falsehood as represented by the Black Knight.

The care with which the White Knight is presented on his rare appearances is worth noting. When the White Queen's Pawn is forsaken in 'a cause So strong in truth and equity . . . Poor harm-less Innocence art thou left a prey To the devourer?', it is the White Knight who alone takes her part: 'No thou art not lost . . . If the fair policy I aim at prospers'. But he is followed not only by his companion the White Duke but also by the White Bishop's Pawn her lover: 'Let it be my honour, sir, Make me that flight that owes her my life's service' (II.2.239 ff). For the moment political issues are forgotten in the plight of an innocent girl abducted by evil powers against which her lover's strength is inadequate, and succoured by a champion of superhuman quality. When the White Pawn is rescued it is with the terms of chivalry that the White King welcomes him.

> Noble chaste Knight . . .
> This fair delivering Act virtue will register
> In that white book of the defence of Virgins
> Where the clear fame of all preserving knights
> Are to eternal memory consecrated.
>
> [III.1.158]

After this it is impossible to see the White Knight's later exploit as other than a deed of chivalry. The political implications are of course still there; to the audience at the Globe this is the heir to the throne so nearly involved with a power alien in every respect to Protestant hearts, but he is also a figure of Spenserian romance, a Red Cross Knight doing battle for his Una, the rep-resentation of truth, against the Serpent—'The glittering'st Serpent that ever falsehood fashioned'.

Considering the shock of delight which we know greeted the actual appearance on stage of Gondamar's chair of ease and perhaps a familiar suit of clothes, it is not unlikely that the White Knight, his opposite, was costumed with equal care. Had the White King's words a visual counterpart? Did Middleton expect the resources of the stage wardrobe to be lavished on the White Knight so as to produce an aura of romance?—which would have again been a delicate compliment but one devised with the artist's eye for wider and deeper dimensions of meaning. In fact the play's increasing concern with the strife between truth and falsehood may owe a good deal to the influence of Spenser.

It is hardly surprising that a poet of Milton's Puritan sympathies should have read this play with interest. He probably had it in mind during the writing of *Lycidas* where there is the clearest verbal echo.[16] Whether or not he also had the play in mind during the conception of *Comus*, the affinity between the two is worth considering. Like the White Queen's Pawn in an alien environment the Lady embodies chastity, and Middleton's heroine expresses her imperviousness to sensual desires in words which Milton's Lady might have spoken:

> I've only in the dignity of the creature
> Admir'd the maker's glory.
>
> [I.1.183]

But less like Milton than Webster when he conceived his Duchess, Middleton could not do otherwise than link his ideal of virtue with feminine beauty. Here, perhaps for the first time to such a degree, he found an excuse to lavish his lyrical power not only on girlhood, but also on holiness itself.

> Upon those lips, the fresh sweet buds of youth,
> The holy dew of prayer lies, like pearl
> Dropt from the opening eyelids of the morn
> Upon the bashful rose.
>
> [I.1.77]

The 'blessed spring' of living water, the 'sacred temple' and the 'sacred altar' are associated with her, and in one of the loveliest lines Middleton ever penned, she is linked in her bashfulness, with

> A vestal virgin in a slip of prayer.
>
> [I.1.146]

There is a degree of correspondence here with two aspects of Milton's Lady: the beauty with which, according to current neo-Platonic idealism, the mind's innocence can invest the body, and the armour of chastity—'She that hath that is clad in complete steel'.

Again the debate between Comus and the Lady, in which the latter praises the simple life, is in the spirit of the Pawn's determination to 'force nothing from its proper nature'; her code of behaviour allows for no anticipation of pleasure or advantage, and it is with the wisdom of humility that she rebukes her own desire to foresee the future:

> O I did ill to give consent to see it! . . .
> Our wills are like a cause that is law-tost,
> What one court orders is by another crost.
>
> [III.2.56]

With this the Lady's condemnation of self-will has some affinity, but in contrast the White Queen's Pawn cannot dogmatise; for Middleton morality is instinctive rather than rational and as the Black Queen's Pawn observes, though with a sinister intention, 'We do not always feel the faith we live by, Nor ever see our growth' (III.1.338). The White Queen's Pawn is an innocent character, not a projection, as is Milton's Lady, of a particular aspect of innocence; she is therefore more easily conceived within the appropriately lyrical context of a lovely and lovable personage. But she is the more vulnerable. Whereas for Milton, chastity is supernaturally armed here, as an interesting modification, innocence carries with it its own flaw. It is her innocence that exposes her to chicanery where equivocal argument has failed, and the Black Bishop's taunt that she is now mere 'brokage', though false, is a reminder that had she yielded as she intended, on a pre-contract, not even the White Knight could have saved her. She is preserved not by her virtue, but by her enemies' lust which drives them to prey on one another, and her subsequent vow of virginity has a disturbing but very human logic. Again, in contrast to Milton, Middleton develops his theme on a convincing commonplace level. Milton's imagination plays round an embodied quality and in this, perhaps the most lyrical of his early compositions, the selective nature of his purpose, coupled with his own immaturity, leaves his Lady largely unrealised. Thus the climax of Milton's work is a debate, not a dramatic episode. Nevertheless the identification in the debate of power with lust has yet another parallel with the moral scheme of this play.

Hitherto Middleton had dissociated lust from acquisitiveness. Allwit is no sensualist, Whorehound is not led by greed; the desire that motivates De Flores is expressed in intellectual rather than physical terms. There are, in fact, few sensualists as such until we come to Livia in *Women Beware Women*, but even in that play the Duke's seduction of Bianca is largely an exercise of will. But here lechery, aggrandisement and dissembling are linked in the Fat Bishop, the Black Bishop's Pawn and the Black King, as they are linked in Comus, who woos the Lady with threats like those which momentarily frighten the White Queen's Pawn, with magic arts which, like the White Queen's Pawn at one point, she despises, and with a power of illusion which bears some resemblance to the arts practised on the White Knight and his companion in the Black House.

That Middleton should build a political satire round a theme which was to inspire a Puritan moralist, is some indication of the direction in which his mind and art were moving. It would be unfair to compare the young Milton with the mature Middleton, or to look for the three-dimensional approach of the play in a masque intended for sophisticated entertainment. But the affinity between the two works serves to underline a frankness of moral conviction which Middleton had not permitted himself earlier, and with this, an ability to apply such conviction without destroying the integrity of character, an achievement which some of his younger contemporaries were to fall short of in the coming neo-Platonic drama of the Caroline theatre.

The White Queen's Pawn's qualities are impressive precisely because, however sketchily, we see them embodied in a vulnerable and fallible person. The young girl's fragility, which is nevertheless so hard to break, is the core of the play's intention. The use of failed purpose, whether good or bad, to imply a moral standpoint, instead of the detached commentators of earlier work demonstrates a new economy and dramatic control. For Middleton in *A Game at Chess*, the ultimate triumph of White over Black is a foregone conclusion, but the issue is effectively illumined by the unavailing penitence of the Black Knight's Pawn. Of all the avowed lechers in the play it is the relatively unimportant pawn who repents. Seeking vainly for counsel in his confessor, half envying the tougher conscience of his master, he stands helpless before the representatives of Church and State, the Fat Bishop and the Black Knight. With the defencelessness of ignorance he describes himself: 'I scarce can read, I was brought up in blindness'. Yet it is he alone of the Black House who thinks the Jesuit's worldly dress a 'strange habit for a holy father'; but his training has taught him not to hold opinions.

> But we, the sons and daughters of obedience
> Dare not once think awry . . .
>
> [IV.1.8]

Milton's indictment in *Lycidas* that 'the hungry sheep look up and are not fed' is well illustrated in this spectacle of a weak and self-wrung penitent pleading for absolution and penance while the Fat Bishop unconcernedly flicks the pages of the Taxa Poenitentiaria. This is more than the projection of a moral philosophy, more too than political satire; it is a denunciation of 'blind Mouths' in any age and of the plight of little men who depend on them for want of better guides.

I do not wish to overstress the moral aspect of what was, more immediately, a topical satire. The moral implication is there, the result of what appears to be a strongly felt conviction, and I have already suggested that the core of the plot may have been growing in Middleton's mind for some time before the actual date of writing. Nevertheless he wrote for an immediate purpose and it was certainly topical interest that drew the audience at the Globe. But Middleton was a master of innuendo, and the two-fold nature of the play enriches the writing as well as the content. This is in many ways the most poetic of Middleton's greater works, and the use of dramatic imagery is one of its many links with *Women Beware Women*.[17]

As far as we know Middleton did not keep a notebook; before *Women Beware Women* there is no evidence that he was at all systematic in looking for figurative means of emphasis and development, as was Webster. Imagery with Middleton is usually unobtrusive and seldom used for immediate effect; but here there is some conscious use of extended imagery, like a musical accompaniment, to develop the impression of a personality. Attention has already been drawn to the images filling out the impression of the White Queen's Pawn, and when we come to the satirical figures the imagery is rich in double meaning. The Fat Bishop inspires a number of imaginative concepts, often extended in the manner of parable, as are several passages already noted in *Women Beware Women*. At his first entrance he applies to himself a triple image which builds up both a moral significance and a physical impression. He is great, he says,

> Much like the lady in the lobster's head,
> A great deal of shell and garbage of all colours,
> But the pure part that should take wings and mount,
> Is at last gasp; as if a man should gape,
> And from his huge bulk let forth a butterfly,
> Like those big-bellied mountains which the poet
> Delivers, that are brought to bed with mouse-flesh.
>
> [II.2.5]

The moral is succinct enough; the woman, the butterfly, the man, all concealed in the worthless mass, build up the sense of futility. But more important is the implication of grossness in 'garbage', 'huge bulk', 'big-bellied', 'brought to bed'; the Fat Bishop's sensuality is given away in manner and tone as it might be in life. The lines are directed against himself, but the point of the passage is that no one but he could speak them.

By another series of analogies and with the same eye to character, the whole outlook of the Black Bishop's Pawn is clarified in the following dialogue. The White Queen's Pawn demurring at his illicit suggestion exclaims:

> If this be virtue's path, 'tis a most strange one:
> I never came this way before.
>
> BL. B.P.:   That's your ignorance;
> And therefore shall that idiot still conduct you
> That knows no way but one, nor ever seeks it?
> If there be twenty ways to some poor village
> 'Tis strange that virtue should be put to one.
>
> [II.1.76]

This careful application of the image, apt at every point and developed with obvious deliberation, is peculiar to *A Game at Chess*. It is not her ignorance but her moral sense that is the idiot

in his eyes; the poor village with its village idiot is the simplicity of
innocence which he repudiates, while the twenty ways suggest
the latitude he tries to persuade her to. The whole passage with
its scorn of simplicity is vibrant with the irritation which will
break out into open threats a few lines later; it implies a complexity of feeling and prejudice, yet the ideas crowd round a clear,
straightforward impression of a typical country village, with the
vividness of parable.

But the imagery connected with the Black Knight is more succinct. Contrast with the passages already quoted, the vivid
evocation of the

> . . . leviathan-scandal that lies rolling
> Upon the crystal waters of devotion.
>
> [II.2.169]

Like the passage quoted above describing the locusts on the ears
of corn, this has the touch of the grotesque which always accom-
panies imagery used by the Black Knight. As a vehicle of satire
its skill lies in the contrast between the impression of purity in
the second line quoted, with that of grossness and misplacement
in the first. A similar economy and careful selection of the significant word has an incisive effect in such lines as (my italics):

> My soul *bleeds* at mine eyes.
>
> [I.1.6]
>
> Nor with my refined nostrils *taste* the footsteps
> Of any of my disciples.
>
> [*Induction*: 3]

This loving attention to words, this savouring of the sound of a
phrase and the image it conveys, is a comparatively late development in Middleton's work, but it is strangely accompanied in this
play by some skilful use of epigrammatic, sometimes rhyming,
couplets, which pinpoint a moral situation in a manner suggestive
of the dramatist's own viewpoint and foreshadow the satirical
and philosophic verse of the 18th Century. For instance the White
Queen's Pawn gravely rebukes herself after looking in the magic
glass:

> What certainty is in our blood or state?
> What we still write is blotted out by fate.
>
> [III.2.57]

—and the Black Queen's Pawn exhorts her in an observation which the latter admits was 'well applied':

> We do not always feel the faith we live by,
> Nor ever see our growth, yet both work upward.
>
> [III.1.338]

In the history of Jacobean dramatic poetry the play looks both forwards and backwards; it is nevertheess a whole in conception and in feeling.

However we place *A Game at Chess* in relation to Middleton's other work, much of what he had done hitherto reached a culmination here and it is regrettable that he did not carry its potential into further writing for the stage. Middleton's last three plays are a sustained exercise in discipline and their detachment and objectivity are something that a modern dramatist might envy. Few artists have trained their eyes more steadily upon the fact, few dramatists have said so much about life and recorded so little of themselves. But allegory, like the dream, is the imagination's natural outlet; as we follow this cleverly contrived fable we seem, occasionally, to catch the poet off his guard. Beatrice, Bianca and Isabella are the creations of his reason, the White Queen's Pawn in the projection of a half expressed idealism.

Yet his handling of moral issues is still characteristically reticent. With Middleton evil is never overcome by good. The White Queen's Pawn repudiates love, not in loyalty to her disabled lover, but in revulsion from those who have deceived her. Middleton had no room for an Héloise even in this type of play, for an ideal love whatever his own conviction, had no relevance to the experience of average humanity which inspired his work in serious drama, and in which the comic and the tragic constantly met and fused. The urge to find a suitable vehicle for that fusion of opposites, which was basic to his irony, had been an impulse to growth since the writing of *A Chaste Maid in Cheapside*, and as we have seen, in *Women Beware Women* the fusion failed.

For R. B. Parker, Middleton's problem lay in reconciling the polarities of 'comic vitality' and of a Calvinistic sense of retribution, particularly in the later comedies and in *Women Beware Women*.[18] This it seems to me is another way of describing the complementary aspects of Middleton's dual vision of life. But in itself this was less a 'problem' than what, as an artist, he was constantly trying to express. It was the essential contradiction at the heart of the human comedy. In the plays it is when the weak and the mediocre face their destiny that they also come to know their limitations, and in that knowledge to attain a momentary dignity only enhanced by the touch of absurdity in their situation. It is then that they become objects, not of pity, certainly never of admiration, but of a common concern.

What kind of play would Middleton have produced had he written more? Would he have retrieved the partial failure of *Women Beware Women*? Does the Pawns' plot derive from a preliminary sketch for a new kind of serious play—perhaps a tragicomedy—which he had no opportunity to write? As they stand the characters and the pattern suggested in the action are of course only sketched in outline, but there are in embryo some surprisingly new elements which ask for development. The White Queen's Pawn is not only a curious combination of Jane Russell's sturdy integrity with Isabella's childlike receptiveness, she is also a first example in Middleton of innocence in its pejorative sense; the untried virtue that protects her can also lay her open to betrayal. The unpredictable in the human factor is a major interest in the Pawns' story. De Flores is surprised but not thrown off balance when he encounters the unfamiliar, but the bewilderment of the Black Bishop's Pawn confronted with the White Pawn's innocence shakes his whole personality. More interesting still is the promise of complexity in the unhappy penitent caught, in the focus of the play, fleeing from the tensions of conscience and desire. The treatment of the Pawns suggests deeper contrarieties of character which if developed might make their own moral challenge on a realistic or psychological level. Instead of the detached moral exponents of the tragedies, here we have the master of policy to rebuke and exhort with sardonic comment, an expert in discretion. As Octavius is to Brutus, the Black Knight is potentially the judgment of the world upon those who are too good for it. Drawn as a straight character in a different kind of plot, such a figure might have eliminated both the retributive justice and the classic catastrophe which confuse the ending of *Women Beware Women*.

Perhaps no dramatist of the period other than Shakespeare knew more about the impact of one character upon another, both as a shaping force in drama and as a basic factor in the human

intercourse which informs it. But reading through Middleton's
last three plays one is often conscious of a holding back from
something like the profound tragic experience of Shakespeare's
mature period. To have explored that experience through the
type of character Middleton chose to create, with the disciplined
observation which his long training had brought him, would have
opened up new possibilities in serious drama; it might also have
helped to bridge the gap between Jacobean and post-Restoration
tragedy.

In the event Middleton stands alone, with a mature output
insufficient to justify as serious innovation what may well have
seemed to contemporaries aberration or mere uncertainty. The
coincidence of his last three plays with cultural and social develop-
ments which were to affect the Caroline theatre was perhaps
unfortunate. Webster's tragic period was over, Ford and Mas-
singer were on the scene, neo-Platonism and the theories of
Burton, modified to the taste of a coterie, would soon dominate
the stage. But to Middleton the drama was still, as it had been to
Shakespeare, the mirror of life. To maintain the spirit of English
drama against the coming decadence a re-thinking of the meaning and scope of tragedy was required. We have seen Middleton
feeling his way through citizen comedy and social satire towards
a fresh tragic formula; paradoxically it was precisely his understanding of the ironic comedy inherent in human existence that
shaped his conception of tragedy during the twenties. But it
needed time and sustained professional purpose to define it—
and Middleton had neither.[19]

As his work stands Middleton impresses his readers but satisfies
none; it is an unfinished achievement. That the (probable) final
offering should have been no more to his contemporaries than a
notorious success and a popular best seller, with so great a
promise of coming strength, is the more regrettable. As it is we are
left with a kind of wisdom, a compassion which never extenuates
and a humour which assesses without belittling. Middleton has
been called in germ 'the Ibsen of the seventeenth Century'; in
the play he did not write he could have anticipated the moderns.

Appendix
The Date of *Women Beware Women*

PROFESSOR Oliphant dates this play late in Middleton's life; more recently Schoenbaum links it with *The Changeling* on grounds of affinity in style and outlook (*Middleton's Tragedies* p. 102 f). Both plays borrow from *The Spanish Curate*, but considering Middleton's well-known and unpredictable repetitiveness this evidence is of limited value. The play's maturity of style and thinking would rule out the possibility of a date earlier than that of *The Changeling*.

The Changeling must have been written some time between the date of its source, published in 1621, and its performance at Court in January 1623; some time in the later months of 1622 is the usually accepted date. *A Game at Chess* we know was first performed on August 6th, 1624. It follows that *Women Beware Women* must fall either between late 1622 and August 1624 or between 1624 and June/July 1627, the date of Middleton's death.

There are those who would place *Women Beware Women* earlier than *The Changeling*.[1] Development in *Women Beware Women* of the episodes of temptation or deception first used in *A Fair Quarrel* and *The Changeling* have been noted. But the temptation of the White Queen's Pawn in *A Game at Chess* is built upon a new element—that of equivocation. Equivocation may be suggested in the nature of the theme, but the chess game in *Women Beware Women* with its ironic *double entendre* could well be a first sketch for the main conception of *A Game at Chess*. The story of the White Queen's Pawn is that of Bianca *in reverse*, a modification which suggests closeness in date, since it is scarcely conceivable that an experienced dramatist would repeat the plot of a known play unmodified, unless after some interval though he might do so in a different guise, especially under pressure of time. Again between *The Changeling* and *A Game at Chess* there is a noticeable growth in complexity of characterisation. In contrast to the slightly flattened characterisation of *The Changeling*, the major characters in *Women Beware Women* are presented in the round, though with less complexity than is suggested in outline in the Pawns' plot. In *A Game at Chess* Middleton seems to reach a new phase in characterisation, to which he had been moving in *Women Beware Women*.

The developed allegorical image which Middleton had begun to use in *Women Beware Women* is employed in *A Game at Chess* in a form approximating to the epic simile. In Leantio's triple image in the lines on 'honest wedlock' (*Women Beware Women* II.1.89f.) subject and image are held apart while the impression is strengthened by an accumulation of analogies; in the Fat Bishop's lines on the lady in the lobster's head, (*Game at Chess*, II.2.5 f.) in the comparison of the same character to the 'blind mole' in the earth (IV.8.9) subject and image seem to identify in a double series of impressions developing simultaneously. There is an artifice in the imagery of *A Game at Chess* which, discounting the demands of political and moral satire, seems to mark a development since *The Changeling*, in which *Women Beware Women* occupies a transitional phase.

All this is guesswork, but there is another possible clue in Middleton's echoing of *The Duchess of Malfi* in the three plays. Recollections of *The Duchess of Malfi* in *The Changeling* are such as might be retained from witnessing a stage performance; for example the madmen's dance and the dead man's finger may recall the mask of madmen and the dead man's hand of Webster's play; there are few verbal echoes and of those the outstanding example 'Come rise and shroud your blushes in my bosom' (*Changeling*, III.4.167) reproduces a line which many theatre-goers might remember—'O let me shroud my blushes in your bosom' (*Duchess of Malfi*, I.1.574). The parallel passages in *Women Beware Women*, though little more numerous than those in *The Changeling* could very well result from close familiarity with the text. For example:

1. Sin and I'm acquainted . . .

[II.2.44]

I am acquainted with sad misery . . .

[*Duchess of Malfi*, IV.2.29]
(Both passages convey the idea that 'custom makes it easy'.)

2. My heart flames for it . . .

[II.1.238]

Mine (heart) bleedes for it.

[*Duchess of Malfi*, III.2.123]

3. What burnt the valley came first from the hill.

[IV.1.215]

There's no deep valley but near some great hill.

[*Duchess of Malfi*, II.5.169]

4. My soul stands ready at my lips.

[V.1.238]

I hold my weary soul in my teeth . . .

[*Duchess of Malfi*, V.4.94]

Now *The Duchess of Malfi* was still popular in the theatre in 1622 but it was not published until towards the end of 1623, so that while Middleton probably knew the play in the theatre by the date of *The Changeling*, he could have had access to the text in 1623.

In *A Game at Chess* the only likely borrowings from Webster as far as I can discover, are three from *The Duchess of Malfi*:

1. Me-thinks I stand over a powder-vault
    And the match now a-kindling.

                                                        [II.1.159]

        I stand
    As if a mine beneath my feet were ready
    To be blown up.

                                    [*Duchess of Malfi*, III.2.186]

2. Integrity of life is so dear to me ...

                                                        [III.1.273]

    Integrity of life is fame's best friend ...

                                    [*Duchess of Malfi*, V.5.145]

and (3) the Black Queen's Pawn's assurance that after a pre-contract 'Y'are man and wife, all but Church ceremony' (IV.1.145) which may owe something to the Duchess's assertion after her own contracting before a witness: 'What can the Church force more?' (I.1.569).

It seems therefore that Middleton had been able to absorb the text of *The Duchess of Malfi* before writing *Women Beware Women*, and the number of parallel passages in that play compared with those in *A Game at Chess* may suggest a certain excitement over a newly published play which abated somewhat towards the latter half of 1624.

These parallels are of course no more than contributory evidence Admittedly to date *Women Beware Women* after *A Game at Chess* would give a neater, in some respects more logical spread to Middleton's mature work, but I cannot feel that this is the true picture. My surmise—and it can only be surmise—is that *Women Beware Women* was written late in 1623 or early in 1624, and that *A Game at Chess* followed fairly closely upon it, not from choice but from necessity.

Notes

Chapter 1

[1] T. S. Eliot, *Elizabethan Dramatists*, [1927] edn. 1962, pp. 84 and 93.

[2] T. B. Tomlinson, *A Study of Elizabethan and Jacobean Tragedy*, p. 175.

[3] Mark Eccles, *Review of English Studies*, VII, Oct. 1931, pp. 431–41.

[4] H. Dugdale Sykes, *Notes and Queries*, June 20th, 1925, p. 435.

[5] Recent authorities date this play as late as 1616; others would place it at approximately 1607. In style and general attitude this is where it would seem to belong. The problem is summarised by G. E. Bentley, who favours a date about 1616, in *The Jacobean and Caroline Stage*, p. 902.

On the other hand the number of characters, few of which could be doubled, the frequency of songs and intervals for music, suggest that the play was originally intended for a Children's company. If so, it must have been written before 1609. References to *The Scornful Lady* of 1612 (I.2), and the Overbury scandal of 1615 (V.1) are topical allusions which might well be inserted in a revival.

[6] Middleton and Rowley had collaborated already in *The Old Law* of 1606.

[7] See W. D. Dunkel—'Did not Rowley merely revise Middleton?', *Publications of the Modern Language Association*, XLVIII pp. 800–2). On the other hand N. W. Bawcutt would assign to Rowley a good deal of *The Changeling*. (See p. 51, note 2–Ch. 4.)

[8] *The Spanish Gipsy*, probably first performed in 1623, was published as by Middleton and Rowley in 1653. But in 1923 H. Dugdale Sykes attributed it entirely to Ford (*Sidelights on Elizabethan Drama*, Chap. IX). It is possible that Rowley had some share in the play, but if Middleton contributed anything it was no more than the sketchiest revision.

[9] See Appendix note on The Date of *Women Beware Women*, p. 125–7.

[10] Quoted by R. C. Bald from the State Papers of James I, in his 1929 edition of *A Game at Chess*, Appendix A, p. 162.

[11] S. Schoenbaum includes *The Mayor of Queenborough* of about 1606 among Middleton's tragedies and would also attribute to him *The Revenger's Tragedy* which he identifies with a lost play by Middleton, *The Viper and her Brood*. (See *Middleton's Tragedies*, 1955, pp. 166ff.)

Chapter 2

[1] A. Harbage, *Shakespeare and the Rival Traditions*, pp. 41ff.

[2] *The Widow* was published in 1652 under the authorship of Jonson, Fletcher and Middleton. Havelock Ellis notes, however, that in a copy of the Quarto, formerly in the possession of Dyce, the names of Jonson and Fletcher are scored through and the word 'alone' written in a possibly contemporary hand, after that of Middleton. (See Mermaid Series, *Thomas Middleton*, Vol. II, p. 394.) The play is so much a whole that it seems un-

reasonable to attribute it to three hands without clear textual evidence. There is little in style or content to suggest the work of either of Middleton's supposed collaborators, with the exception of the episode of Latrocino's quack doctoring (IV.2) which may be modelled on a scene from Jonson's *Volpone* (but see following note), and some traces of Fletcher's influence which are noted below.

³ Miss W. Smith, in her *The Commedia dell'Arte* of 1911, believes the episode of Latrocino's quack doctoring in *The Widow*, as also the mountebank scene in Jonson's *Volpone*, on which she believes it may be modelled, to be based on Commedia dell'Arte material.

⁴ Cf. Amintor's scruples of conscience which complicate an already painful dilemma in *The Maid's Tragedy*, the divided loyalties which Maximus discovers in himself in *Valentinian* (written entirely by Fletcher), and the tender sensibilities which grow up in the triangular relationship between Philaster, Bellario and Arethusa in *Philaster*.

It is of interest that Middleton follows up this episode with the still more idealistic story of Captain Ager's troubles of conscience in *A Fair Quarrel* of 1615.

⁵ The episode of Bellafront's recovery in *The Honest Whore* would, of course, be an exception, but this is probably the work of Dekker.

⁶ This is a favourite comic situation in 17th Century drama. For instance Jonson makes use of it in reverse in *Volpone* (IV.1.) where Lady Politick Would-be mistakes Peregrine for a woman in disguise.

⁷ Phoenix is another advocate of the married state. As detached spectator, however, his utterances remain on the level of comment, and are scarcely to be taken as part of the theme.

⁸ An exception is the scene following the christening feast, where the situation in the Allwit household is clearly parodied in Touchwood Senior's ministrations to the childless and quarrelsome Sir Oliver and Lady Kix, 'the barren he and she'. It's significance depends as much on Touchwood's confidences to the audience as on the couple's bland innocence.

> Here is a little vial of almond milk,—
> (Aside) That stood me in some threepence,

[III.3.90]

and when the quarrel recommences:

> By this light they're out again
> At the same door, and no man can tell which way. (Aside)

[III.3.99]

⁹ S. Schoenbaum, *Studies in the English Renaissance Drama*, p. 298. Schoenbaum notes of this comedy that it is the wittol who takes the place of the moral exponents of the earlier plays.

¹⁰ For instance, the fortunes of Ricardo have something of the folk–tale justification of the poor boy in luck, while Middleton's numerous mild-tempered husbands—invariably a little slow-witted—and their perpetual conflict with quick-witted wives have a kinship with the rivalry of the goodman and his dame in the ballad 'Get up and Bar the Door'.

¹¹ This sharp change of tone is not unlike that effected at the death of Brachiano in Webster's tragedy, *The White Devil* (V.3.) when the dying man's 'assistants' throw off their disguise and reveal themselves as his murderers. There is a possible verbal parallel in Sir Walter's question: 'What's he knows now How long I have to live?'—recalling Flamineo's similar appeal to the ghost of Brachiano immediately after this episode: 'is

it in your knowledge To answer mee how long I have to live?' (V.4.123)
If Middleton had this scene in mind, his own would read like a deliberate
parody. The parallel, whether conscious or not, emphasises some new
elements in this play.

12 The name was popularly associated with the sparrow, the prototype of
lust, a significance to which Middleton draws attention at III.2.25—'a
cock-sparrow that will come at Philip'.

13 On the other hand R. B. Parker notes that Middleton's habit of
presenting several sets of characters 'of almost equal importance revolving
round a central character' has the opposite effect in that it reduces the
impression of 'solemnity'. (*Stratford-upon-Avon Studies*, I, 1960, p. 185.)
Perhaps the truth is that Middleton's fertility in plot device can arouse a
complexity of response in the audience and allow for multiple shades of
interpretation.

14 Mistress Lucre's jealousy on behalf of her slow-witted son, whom she
orders to relinquish his suit for the hand of Joyce in favour of the widow,
would have served Witgood's purpose as a lover. Thus if her plot had been
allowed to materialise the play would have turned on a romantic interest
rather than on the trickery which, as it stands, is its major concern. If
Middleton already had the draft of such a play he could well have utilised
it, perhaps at short notice, modified in its present form in order to suit the
less sentimental requirements of the audience at St. Paul's. It is easy to
overwork the theory of revision but that seems a possible explanation.

15 If at some stage in the history of the play, rather more musical interludes than appear in the text at present were required for the use of a boys'
company, Susan may have had her uses as a musical companion for Moll.
We hear of Moll's music lessons in the first scene, but she performs only on
her supposed deathbed.

Chapter 3

1 See p. 51, note 2 and p. 57, note 7—Ch. 4. In *A Fair Quarrel* both hands
seem discernible intermittently throughout the text, although most critics
assign the Chough-Trimtram passages mainly to Rowley. My own guess is that
while each revised the other's work Middleton was the dominant partner.

2 It is unusually difficult to distinguish between the two hands in this
scene. Middleton seems to open the play, but there are possible traces of
Rowley even, here and there, in passages which one would assign to
Middleton. The final section after the withdrawal of the friends seems to
be mainly Rowley's work and, as often happens in Middleton-Rowley plays,
Rowley probably handled the passages of physical action, such as the two
altercations and the bustle surrounding the arrest. But all this is guesswork
and though varied, the episode is without obvious transitions.

3 The closest parallel is in *Women Beware Women* (II.1) where Livia
betrays Isabella into incest with her uncle by persuading her in a series
of feigned hesitations that she is of no kin to him. But there is a similarly
slow rise of tension as Beatrice gradually comes to understand the precise
nature of De Flores' claim upon her when he comes to report the success
of their joint plan to murder Alonso (*The Changeling*. III.4).

4 Middleton is non-committal as to the morality of consummating marriage
on a pre-contract. This was a contemporary problem in ethics which

Shakespeare had touched upon in *Measure for Measure*. Middleton would return to it in his ambiguous treatment of the situation in *A Game at Chess* where the White Queen's pawn seems ready to accept her lover on a pre-contract but is manifestly relieved when he fails to keep the assignation. Since the lover is the would-be seducer in disguise the inference is that Middleton's attitude was generally orthodox.

5 The similarity in manner between the two episodes lends some support to the view that, although Rowley has been credited with much of the comic matter, the conception of the play as a whole was mainly from Middleton. (See A. G. Swinburne, Introduction, *Thomas Middleton*, ed. Havelock Ellis, Mermaid Series, pp. xx–xxi.)

6 The witty dialogue in this scene is in Rowley's manner, but it makes a useful preparation for the temptation scene (III.2) which was probably mainly Middleton's work.

7 See *Thomas Middleton* Vol. II, ed. Havelock Ellis, Mermaid Series, p. 271, footnote.

8 See p. 54, note 5—Ch. 4—and p. 88, note 6—Ch. 5.

Chapter 4

1 N. W. Bawcutt remarks of this passage: 'It is perhaps ironical that the fullest statement of the "sight" and "judgment" theme is by Beatrice herself, and it sums up the play as fully as any single quotation can do.' (*The Changeling*, Revels Plays, p. xlvi.)

2 Rowley is usually credited with the opening and closing scenes and the comic sub-plot and Middleton with the rest of the main plot. In my view Middleton had a good deal to do with the sub-plot also, while Rowley seems to have revised the opening and closing scenes; Rowley's hand is certainly discernible in V.1. The authors seem to have worked in close sympathy but I would assume that Middleton was responsible for the overall conception.

3 Alsemero's closet with its preparations designed to test a woman's chastity may be another vestige of the husband's jealousy. Surprising as this form of pleasantry may be in association with Alsemero, Middleton, re-membering his sources, may intend to suggest by it, not only that the bridegroom could be jealous, but rather that his ideal of the married state may be more than Beatrice can respond to.

4 The obvious comparison is with the plight of Amintor in *The Maid's Tragedy* (see comment p. 40). But whereas Evadne's ruthless admission that she is the King's mistress, and her subsequent equally violent repentance wring the sympathy on Amintor's behalf out of a totally unreal situation, Middleton's ironic sense of humour almost persuades us to accept that of Beatrice and Alsemero as something from life.

5 In both scenes the tempter plays upon the victim with calculated skill until her innocence gives him the opening that he seeks. Like Jane Beatrice is concerned with the problem of rewarding the man she has used and like Jane she passes from bewilderment to outrage. More important is the strong emphasis in *The Changeling* on the word 'deed' which recalls the verbal play on the same word in the scene in *A Fair Quarrel*: 'Indeed I love you ... What deed? ... The deed that you have done' (III.2.97).

6 See *The Duchess of Malfi* (IV.1.). Webster may have had in mind the superstition connected with the Hand of Glory, the dead man's hand with

which thieves were said to cast a spell over the householder while they ransacked his goods.

⁷ Act V, sc.1. This is a problem scene, but while it is among the most effective in the play it also illustrates the closeness with which Middleton and Rowley could collaborate. Beatrice's nervous tension, cynically watched by De Flores, is characteristic of Middleton, but the violent action in the latter half of the scene is most likely from Rowley.

The use of a fire to distract attention recalls Rowley's *A Shoemaker a Gentleman* in which Crispianus causes a tree to be set on fire that the populace may mistake it for a beacon signalling invasion, in order that under cover of the general confusion Leodice, who is with child by him, may escape from the court for her confinement. The parallel with Beatrice's situation is obvious. The noisy bustle of the fire, the clanging of the alarm bell, the call for 'hooks, buckets, ladders', may again be from Rowley whose plays abound in such vigorous action, while there are few comparable passages in the unaided work of Middleton.

On the other hand there is evidence of Rowley's hand—perhaps in the way of revision—at line 13 when in answer to De Flores' question as to whether Diaphanta has returned Beatrice replies: 'As I'm a living soul not.' This usage is strange to Middleton, but there are several examples of it in *A Shoemaker a Gentleman*:

> ALBON: But I'm an Englishmen.
> MAXIMUS: Yet substitute to Rome.   ALBON: Not.
>
> [II.2.54]
>
> CRISPIANUS: I trouble you Madam.   LEODICE: Not.
>
> [II.3.121]
>
> LEODICE: Shall I not need to fear thee?   CRISPIANUS: Not.
>
> [II.3.189]

The section in which the ghost appears seems to be indisputably Middleton's work, yet it is pertinent to recall the skilfully contrived scene in the fatal chamber in Rowley's *All's Lost by Lust*, where Roderigo faces the ghosts of his offended ancestors. If Middleton conceived the tragic irony of this scene, Rowley may well have grasped and exploited its theatrical potentialities.

⁸ For instance the crucifix which Marcello comments upon a moment before his death, or the rich cloak which Brachiano spreads with an arrogant gesture on refusing a stool at the arraignment of his mistress, which remains in full view of the audience after his own departure.

⁹ Una Ellis-Fermor says of Middleton: 'here was in germ the Ibsen of the seventeenth Century' (*The Jacobean Drama*, p. 152). Professor R. H. Barker notes the affinity with Ibsen as early as *A Fair Quarrel* in 'the tragedy of Lady Ager' (*Thomas Middleton*, p. 109).

¹⁰ Beatrice refers to him as a 'standing toad-pool', and as a viper with which she must engender, and she later asserts that, in association with him, she has 'kiss'd poison'. Tomaso shrinks from him as

> . . . most deadly venomous,
> He would go near to poison any weapon
> That should draw blood upon him.
>
> [V.2.17]

See also M. C. Bradbrook, *Themes and Conventions of Elizabethan Tragedy*, p. 234.

¹¹ Mr. N. W. Bawcutt, among others, notes parallels with Iago (*The Changeling*, Revels Plays, p. xxxiv).

¹² Lodovico declares at the close of *The White Devil* when his revenge is complete: 'I limn'd this night-piece, and it was my best.'

¹³ '. . . fearing De Flores, she (Beatrice) puts him to a practical use to escape him; he could then steal her: she must realise his way of feeling and be dragged into his world. It is . . . the hint of the changeling idea given by the other plot that makes us accept it' (*Some Versions of Pastoral*, p. 52).

¹⁴ Rowley's tragedy *All's Lost by Lust* is a good example. Roderigo's encounter with the spirits on entering the forbidden treasure chamber is managed with such spectacle and rhetoric that we are impressed less by his deservings than by the heroic audacity of his crime.

¹⁵ N. W. Bawcutt notes that the word 'change' occurs nineteen times in the play and 'with a variety of implications' (*The Changeling*, p. xlvii).

¹⁶ Rowley's hand in Act I. sc.1. may be betrayed by the use of the word 'saint': 'I shall change my saint I fear' (I.1.158). This is a Rowley usage, cf. *All's Lost by Lust*,

> ANTONIO: Mars be my morrows Saint.
> LAZARELLO: (indicating Jacintha), Here were a Saint fitting your
>   orisons.
>
>   [I.1.58]

and *A Shoemaker a Gentleman* (II.1.3), where Hugh refers to Winefred whom he loves but may not woo, as 'my interdicted Saint'.

It is also possible that the crude violence of the deaths of Beatrice and De Flores in the closet, their outcries and beating on the locked door, are Rowley additions, for while Middleton's denouements may be clumsy or grotesque they are seldom theatrical in this purely physical way. On the other hand it is Rowley's habit to build up dramatic tension by vigorous action. (See note 7, p. 132.)

Whatever Rowley's share in the sub-plot it seems probable that Middleton devised it as a whole: Alibius and Lollio recall his earlier master and man relationship, Brandino and Martino of *The Widow*, and since Isabella makes so suitable a foil to Beatrice it seems likely that the same mind conceived both characters. Yet Isabella's refreshing good sense may be, like that of Jane in *A Fair Quarrel* from Rowley's influence, and Rowley may have embroidered their story with such characteristic interludes as Isabella's exchanges with Lollio and the light comedy and practical joking of the disguised lovers, all of which recall the pleasant crudity of Rowley's witty lovers.

¹⁷ Isabella's reception of Lollio's sallies and the advances of her admirers is not unlike a situation in Fletcher's play *The Spanish Curate*, in which Amarantha rebuffs the advances of Leandro, her would-be lover, who gains entrance to her husband's house disguised as a shy scholar (II.4). Fletcher's source for this play was a Spanish novel by Gonzalo de Céspedes, translated by Leonard Digges as *The Unfortunate Spaniard*. In fact Mr. Bawcutt (*op. cit.* p. xxxiii), accepts this book as a possible source for the main plot of *The Changeling*, but admits that it could have suggested elements of the sub-plot also. *The Spanish Curate* was probably first acted in 1622.

¹⁸ Compare De Flores' observation on overhearing Beatrice's conversation with Alsemero:

> What shall become of t'other; I'm sure both
> Cannot be serv'd unless she transgress; happily
> Then I'll put in for one.
>
> [II.2.58]

See also M. C. Bradbrook, *Themes and Conventions of Elizabethan Tragedy* p. 221, for comments on parallels between these characters.

[19] Sir Henry Herbert's Office Book includes *The Changeling* in a list of plays performed at Court in 1623.

[20] Professor Oliphant is surely wrong in suggesting that the scene of these festivities was in fact written and subsequently lost (*Shakespeare and his Fellow Dramatists*, p. 203). It is hardly conceivable that a dramatist of Middleton's economy would present the madmen twice with whatever alteration. On the other hand we have no explanation of Alibius's cryptic remark on the purpose of this dance:

> Only an unexpected passage over,
> To make a frightful pleasure, that is all,
> But not the all I aim at.
>
> [II.3.273]

What was the 'all' he aimed at? Did the dramatists originally intend to stage a masque as cover for some act of violence at the wedding feast— a device popular in the contemporary theatre and one which Middleton himself was to use in *Women Beware Women*? Or were these lines intended to prepare the audience for some incident in the final scenes which a change of plan obliged them to dispense with? For Alibius continues:

> ... could we so act it,
> To teach it in a wild distracted measure,
> Though out of form and figure, breaking time's head,
> It were no matter.
>
> [II.3.275]

Was Alibius himself planning some act of satisfaction for the jealousy of which we hear so much? Whatever the original plan the madmen's dance is sufficiently prominent to suggest that it was supposed to be representational and there is an obvious parallel with the masque-like use of madmen in *The Duchess of Malfi* (IV.2).

My own impression is that Rowley was working in close association with Middleton in the passages concerned with the madmen, but that, either in the harassment of completing the play to meet a demand, or in revising it for a Court performance, hasty modifications were made, perhaps during the process of writing.

[21] The importance of the madmen and fools in this use of the sub-plot and the fundamental kinship with Webster's work in the conception of the play is worth noting. See Professor Empson's observation that 'the madhouse dominates every scene; every irony refers back to it; that is why the play is so much nearer Webster than either of its parts' (*Some Versions of Pastoral*, p. 48).

[22] *Op. cit.*, p. lxvi.

[23] S. Schoenbaum, *Middleton's Tragedies*, pp. 25–6.

Chapter 5

1 Middleton's source for this story was probably the *Ducento Novelle* of Coelio Malespino. The tale of Bianco Capello is concluded in Fynes Moryson's *Itinerary*.

2 The original was dated about 1597, and appeared in English as *The True History of the Tragicke Loves of Hipolito and Isabella Neapolitans*. Opinion is divided as to whether Middleton's play was used by the translator or whether Middleton had access to the unpublished MS. (See Roma Gill (ed.), *Women Beware Women*, p. xv for discussion of this matter.)

3 Mr. Schoenbaum's comment that Middleton's characters are 'moral idiots' (*Middleton's Tragedies*, p. 24) will not explain Isabella's total forgetfulness of her initial moral intention when she finds she can entertain a natural love for Hippolyto. The situation has altered and a different interest has taken the stage. I think we must take it that the lapse is not Isabella's but her creator's!

4 *Op. cit.* p. 17, note.

5 E. H. C. Oliphant, *Shakespeare and his Fellow Dramatists*, p. 249.

6 See p. 41, note 3—Ch. 3, where attention is drawn to the first study for this scene, in *A Fair Quarrel* (II.1), where Lady Ager practices deception with a kindlier motive on her son.

7 There is a similar use of a game of chess in Fletcher's *The Spanish Curate* of 1622. Middleton probably knew the play, but it is possible that he also knew Fletcher's own source for the incident in *Gerardo the Unfortunate Spaniard*, a translation of a Spanish novel by G. de Cespedes, published in the same year. In the play Leandro makes love to Amarantha under cover of a game of chess with some *double entendre* on the moves in the game. Meantime the husband is satisfied that the lovers are lawfully occupied at the chessboard.

8 The whole episode has a strong resemblance to the Pawns' story in *A Game of Chess*, where Bianca's trials are restated in reverse. See Appendix ix, The Date of *Women Beware Women*, pp. 125-7.

9 *Op. cit.*, p. 126.

10 At first sight Phoenix may seem an exception. But the play *The Phoenix* is entirely critical in intention and thus Phoenix himself is both the main character and the vehicle of the theme.

Chapter 6

1 Prefixed to an undated Quarto, Bullen's edition 'B'.

2 See R. C. Bald (ed.), *A Game at Chesse*, Introduction.

3 Professor W. Power finds some explanation for this unusual lapse of time between licensing and performance in the possibility that the King was expected to go on progress, a circumstance which would obviously facilitate the presentation of a play likely to offend. More surprising however, is the fact that the play was licensed in the first place, and this Professor Power thinks may be associated with the King's declining health and the ascendancy of Prince Charles. As the White Knight, the Prince is made the centre of the whole conception, and his recent visit to Spain presented in a very

flattering light. Thus while certain persons in authority might reasonably be offended, the play could not fail to please certain others, both at Court and in the country at large. (See 'Thomas Middleton vs. King James I', *Notes and Queries*, Dec. 1957, p. 526 ff.)

⁴ It should be noted however, that the figure of Gondamar may be directly from the engraving on the title page of the second part of *Vox Populi*, Middleton's principal source for the plot, which appeared a little before the play in 1624.

⁵ See letter from Chamberlain to Carleton, 21st Aug. 1624, cited by R. C. Bald: 'they counterfeited his person to the life, with all his graces and faces, and had gotten (they say), a cast suit of his apparell for the purpose . . .'

⁶ Bullen identifies the White King's Pawn with Sir Toby Matthew, son of the Archbishop of York, who became a Jesuit. The suggestion is borne out in the pawn's clerical status, but there the resemblance ends.

⁷ Possibly an allusion to De Dominis' hope of favour from Pope Gregory XV, who had been a personal friend. See R. C. Bald, *op. cit.*, Introduction, p. 9.

⁸ *Church History of Britain*, 1655.

⁹ R. C. Bald, *op. cit.*, quoted in Notes, p. 147.

¹⁰ Bullen seems to ignore both the game of chess and the implications of the play itself in identifying the White Knight with the Duke of Buckingham.

¹¹ R. C. Bald, *op. cit.*, Introduction, p. 17.

¹² *Livia* . . . wives or widows we account ourselves
          Then old, when young men's eyes leave looking at's. II.2.63.

¹³ Romelio, the merchant prince in *The Devil's Law Case*, 1620, and Appius, the lustful power politician of *Appius and Virginia*, written with Thomas Heywood probably in or after 1624.

¹⁴ *The Devil's Law-Case* (III.2.6), ed. F. L. Lucas, 1929.

¹⁵ That the point was noted is suggested in a phrase in the letter from Chamberlain to Carleton, 21st Aug. 1624, quoted above: 'the worst is they played somebody els, for wch they are forbidden to play that or any other play until the Ks. pleasure be known.'

¹⁶   . . . ere the high lawns appeared
          Under the opening eyelids of the morn,
                                        [*Lycidas*, ll. 25–6]
          . . . like pearl
          Dropt from the opening eyelids of the morn.
                                        [*G. at C.*, I.1.78]
The parallel is noted by Dyce and quoted by Bullen. See also R. C. Bald, *op. cit.*, note, p. 139.

¹⁷ See Appendix, The Date of *Women Beware Women*, pp. 125–7.

¹⁸ R. B. Parker, 'Middleton's Experiments with Comedy and Judgment', *Stratford-upon-Avon Studies I* (1960), p. 199.

¹⁹ This would not be the view of D. M. Holmes whose thorough and scholarly examination of Middleton's work as a whole—*The Art of Thomas Middleton* (1970)—came to my notice only after this study had reached completion. Mr. Holmes traces a strongly defined didacticism which he sees underlying Middleton's art and developing steadily to reach a culmination in his mature plays.

In my opinion the moral element in Middleton's work was no more than conventional or tentative until *A Chaste Maid in Cheapside* and reached no definition as part of an artistic purpose until the period of *A Fair Quarrel*.

Appendix

¹ J. I. Cope argues for an early date, 1613–14. (See 'The Date of *Women Beware Women*', *Modern Language Notes*, 76, 1961). R. C. Bald suggests a date a little before 1622 ('The Chronology of Middleton's Plays' *Modern Language Review XXXII*, Jan. 1937), and Baldwin Maxwell would date the play round about 1621 ('The Date of Middleton's *Women Beware Women*', *Philological Quarterly XXII*, 1943). Bentley however would place *Women Beware Women* late and probably after *A Game at Chess* (*The Jacobean and Caroline Stage, Vol. 4* p. 906). The matter is summarised by Roma Gill in *Women Beware Women* (New Mermaids Series), p. xlv.

Bibliography

I. WORKS BY MIDDLETON

A. GENERAL

The Works of Thomas Middleton, ed. A. H. Bullen (8 vols.), London, 1885–6.
The Works of Thomas Middleton, ed. A. Dyce (5 vols.), London, 1840.
Thomas Middleton, ed. Havelock Ellis. (Mermaid Series, 2 vols.), London, 1887–90. This edition contains ten plays.

B. EDITIONS OF SINGLE PLAYS

BALD, R. C. *A Game at Chess*. Cambridge U.P., 1929.
BARBER, C. A. *Trick to Catch the Old One*. (Fountainwell Drama Texts), Oliver & Boyd, 1968.
—— *A Chaste Maid in Cheapside*. (Fountainwell Drama Texts), Oliver & Boyd, 1969.
BAWCUTT, N. *The Changeling*. (Revel Plays), Methuen, 1958.
BRISSENDEN, A. *A Chaste Maid in Cheapside*. (New Mermaids Series), Benn, 1968.
GILL, R. *Women Beware Women*. (New Mermaids Series), Benn, 1968.
HARPER, J. W. *A Game at Chess*. (New Mermaids Series), Benn, 1966.
THOMPSON, P. *The Changeling*. (New Mermaids Series), Benn, 1964.
WATSON, G. *A Trick to Catch the Old One*. (New Mermaids Series), Benn, 1968.

II. OTHER STUDIES

A. BOOKS

BARKER, R. H. *Thomas Middleton*. Columbia U.P., 1958.
BENTLEY, G. E. *The Jacobean and Caroline Stage*. Clarendon Press, 1941–1956.
BRADBROOK, M. C. *Themes and Conventions of Elizabethan Tragedy*. Cambridge U.P., (1935), 1960.
—— *The Growth and Structure of Elizabethan Comedy*. Chatto and Windus, 1955.
ELIOT, T. S. *Elizabethan Dramatists* (1927). Faber (paperback), 1963.
ELLIS-FERMOR, U. M. *The Jacobean Drama* (1936). Methuen, 1958.

EMPSON, WILLIAM, *Some Versions of Pastoral* (1935). Chatto and Windus, 1950.

HARBAGE, ALFRED, *Shakespeare and the Rival Traditions*. Macmillan, New York, 1952.

HOLMES, DAVID M., *The Art of Thomas Middleton*. Oxford U. P., 1970.

KNIGHTS, L. C. *Drama and Society in the Age of Ben Jonson*. Chatto and Windus, 1937.

OLIPHANT, H. C. *Shakespeare and his Fellow Dramatists*. Pitman, 1929.

ORNSTEIN, R. *The Moral Vision of Jacobean Tragedy*. Univ. of Wisconsin Press, 1965.

RIBNER, IRVING. *Jacobean Tragedy*. Methuen, 1962.

SCHOENBAUM, SAMUEL. *Middleton's Tragedies*. Columbia U. P., 1955.

SYKES, H. DUGDALE. *Sidelights on Elizabethan Drama*. Oxford U. P., 1924.

TOMLINSON, T. B. *A Study of Elizabethan and Jacobean Tragedy*. Oxford U. P., 1964.

B. ARTICLES

BALD, R. C. 'The Chronology of Middleton's Plays', *Modern Language Review*, XXXII (Jan., 1937), 33–47.

COPE, J. I. 'The Date of Middleton's *Women Beware Women*', *Modern Language Notes*, 76, 1961.

DUNKEL, W. D. 'Did not Rowley merely revise Middleton?' *Publications of the Modern Language Association*, XLVIII (Sept., 1933), 799–805.

ECCLES, M. 'Middleton's Birth and Education', *Review of English Studies*, VII (Oct., 1931), 431–41.

LEVIN, R. 'The Four Plots of *A Chaste Maid in Cheapside*', *Review of English Studies*, XVI (1965), 14–24.

MAXWELL, B. 'The Date of Middleton's *Women Beware Women*', *Philological Quarterly*, XXII (1943).

PARKER, R. B. 'Middleton's Experiments with Comedy and Judgment' in *Stratford-upon-Avon Studies* (1960): 'Jacobean Theatre'.

POWER, W. 'Thomas Middleton vs King James I', *Notes and Queries* (Dec., 1957), 526 ff.

RICKS, C. 'Word Play in *Women Beware Women*', *Review of English Studies*, XII (1941), 238–50.

SCHOENBAUM, S. '*A Chaste Maid in Cheapside* and Middleton's City Comedy', *Studies in the English Renaissance Drama* (1961), 287–309.

SYKES, H. D. 'Thomas Middleton's Early Non-dramatic Work', *Notes and Queries* (June 20th, 1925).